THE ROAD TO STRANGE

TRAVEL TALES OF THE PARANORMAL AND BEYOND

THE ROAD TO STRANGE

TRAVEL TALES OF THE PARANORMAL AND BEYOND

Michael Brein

and

Rosemary Ellen Guiley

Visionary Living, Inc.
New Milford, Connecticut

The Road to Strange:
Travel Tales of the Paranormal and Beyond

Front cover design by April Slaughter
Back cover and interior design by Leslie McAllister
Illustrations by John Weaver

ISBN: 978-1-942157-15-1 (pbk)
ISBN: 978-1-942157-16-8 (epub)

Published by Visionary Living, Inc.
New Milford, Connecticut
www.visionaryliving.com

Acknowledgements

"You wouldn't believe the incredible stories people have told me about their travels!"

—*Michael Brein*

Thanks to all of you brave souls who have ventured to lands far and wide, and shared your sometimes bizarre, oft frightening, and mostly ineffable, experiences of the paranormal with me for publication. Without you this book could not be written.

Profound thanks to John Weaver for his wonderful illustrations that capture the essence of some of the stories.

Special thanks go to the late Professor Herbert B. Weaver, PhD, former head of the Department of Psychology at the University of Hawaii, without whose mentorship and encouragement I might not have become The Travel Psychologist that I am today.

And finally, thanks to the proprietors of the innumerable unnamed coffee houses that have tolerated me as I sat endlessly working on these stories, hour upon hour with endless refills after refills…

TABLE OF CONTENTS

Preface
Michael Brein

I'm the "The Travel Psychologist." I originally coined the term "Travel Psychology" during my doctoral studies at the University of Hawaii, and then became the world's first travel psychologist.

For five decades, I have crisscrossed and traveled the world numerous times over, interviewing nearly 1,800 travelers and adventurers, and collecting and recording more than 5,000 accounts of all sorts of things that happened to them. I have delved into the deeper psychological aspects of their experiences.

It became apparent during my research that many people got far more than they anticipated from travel – they had unusual experiences of a paranormal, supernatural, and even mystical nature. I saw common themes running through them. These stories fascinated me, and so I began a special collection of them, forging new territory in travel lore that had been ignored and neglected by the mainstream physical or social sciences.

Reading the paranormal travel stories of others presents the reader with new and unique events that are often both eye-opening and awesome – just as travel tends to be itself. It is largely through the novel experiences offered by travel and adventure that we achieve more personal growth and gain an understanding of realities that we perhaps did not know even existed. This aspect of travel is nothing short of a paradigm-shifter.

Travel is mind-opening and mind-bending. Maybe it takes the travel experience – namely the condensing, collapsing, and speeding up of time and space, the rush of novelty, all impacting upon us at once at every turn – to pry open the portals to the unknown. Imagine the degree of impact that a travel-related paranormal event can have on one's life. These events happen to everyone in all walks of life, regardless of belief in the paranormal.

Some of the people in this book acknowledge that they have histories of paranormal and unusual experiences. That is the case with me, as I have had many episodes of premonitions, precognitive dreams, psychic phenomena, and more throughout my life. I call this gift my "Inner Psychic."

Others in this book say they have no extraordinary psychic sense, and some even profess to be skeptical – that is, until their experiences opened their eyes.

The stories in this unique collection are not intended to provide definitive proof of the paranormal. My main purpose is to show that these kinds of experiences not only happen, but they happen often, and, yes, they happen to *you*, and to me, too! I have included a few of my own personal paranormal travel experiences, which "seals the deal," so to speak, for the reality of psychic phenomena, at least for me!

The true stories presented here are a tantalizing mix of topics such as ghosts and hauntings, premonition and precognition, déjà vu, synchronicity, mysticism, spirituality, past lives and reincarnation, clairvoyance, clairaudience, telepathy, black magic, psychic readings, poltergeists, space-time warps, sacred sites, phantom persons, out-of-body experiences, and more. They take place in exotic locations all over the planet, and in all kinds of circumstances.

Reading these stories may help you understand some of the strange events you have encountered in your own travels – and may open you even more to the unknown the next time you venture out.

Perhaps you have a travel story yourself – see the information in the Afterword for how to submit for one of our upcoming volumes.

Before I go, I'd like to share a little more about how this book came into being, something deeply personal to me and which involves an experience like the ones in the stories. It's about "the Aloha Spirit."

In the 1960s, I was studying at Temple University in Philadelphia to become a clinical psychologist, and was offered a full four-year fellowship to complete my PhD. Suddenly, I had enough of the depressing world of mental illness and clinical psychology and decided to make an abrupt career change to become the world's first "travel psychologist." This switch was much to the chagrin of my parents, for the subfield of the "psychology of travel" had not yet come into existence.

My decision meant departing my life on the gloomy East Coast of the U.S. to answer the call of Pacific island breezes, and the sun, surf, and sands of the Hawaiian Islands. By now, in 1965, the travel bug had fully infested me. I was accepted into the PhD program in the Psychology Department of the University of Hawaii, and was awarded a graduate assistantship, which would help with my now uncertain finances.

Perhaps it was a rationalization, but I convinced myself that I should do this so I could study under the tutelage of a former University of Pennsylvania psychology graduate, Herb Weaver, who was now involved in the travel industry of Hawaii, and was also a professor of psychology and the departmental chairman at the University of Hawaii. I became one of his graduate students, and he became my mentor.

We also became quite good friends over time. Completing my doctoral degree at the University of Hawaii was not always perfectly smooth sailing, and I had my share of departmental politics that are probably part and parcel of most graduate students' careers. I'm sure that my professor friend supported me and intervened a few times on my behalf, probably unbeknownst to me.

Eventually my association with Herb took a rocky turn, albeit for a brief period. I got caught up in a situation whereby I selected another faculty member to be the chairman of my dissertation, which angered my professor friend. I thought I was opting for fairness, but I should have made a more politically savvy choice. Herb was trying to run the other professor out of the psychology department.

Herb turned on me briefly. He threatened to "make things difficult" for me and boycotted my important oral defense of my dissertation, the last step of my PhD program. Not attending my oral defense of my thesis was not only a symbolic *pièce de résistance* on his part, but a slap in the face – a supreme insult. He made his point.

Fortunately, things got ironed out. I was supposed to go to his office one day for him to "ask his question" relevant to my defending my dissertation. As I entered his office, the tension in the air could have been cut with a knife. His question was, "Well, what are you going to do now?" That was it! The battle was over; he had made his point; and we were now back to being friends again.

I loved Hawaii so much that I stayed on instead of leaving once I had completed my graduate studies. I didn't keep in touch with Herb after I completed my degree. I knew, however, that he was ailing.

Then one night, I had a dream. It was a lucid dream – real, vivid, and scary. In the dream, I saw a gravestone in a cemetery. I could clearly read a name on the stone: Herbert Weaver. Whoa!

I'd had these sorts of dreams before, prior to the deaths of my parents. I knew full well the meaning of this dream – it was a precognitive dream of impending death. There was no avoiding the stark reality. I knew.

There was more: I was certain that there would be an obituary for Herb in the next day's newspaper, the Sunday morning edition of the *Honolulu Advertiser*. Furthermore, I "knew" with absolute certainty that I would receive a phone call in my Honolulu office from one of my best friends, a former roommate I had when I first arrived in Hawaii, telling me of Herb's death.

I didn't have time on Sunday to search out the obits in the paper, but, just as if on cue, I did receive the phone call on early Monday morning from my friend, Ken, telling me of Herb Weaver's passing over the weekend. For you see, I've had such expected phone calls before in relation to the deaths of a few family members. And indeed, the obituary was in the newspaper as I had surmised.

But there's one more aspect to the story.

Aloha is a Hawaiian word that has a variety of meanings, both as a single word and when used together with other words as well. It is most commonly used as a greeting, meaning "hello," "goodbye," or "farewell." Aloha is also used to mean "love." In addition, it is used to express one's compassion, regret, or even sympathy. So, when someone says "aloha," a lot is wrapped up in that term. I felt that the spirit of my good old friend, Herb Weaver, traveled to me in my dream that night to say one final "aloha," a farewell tinged with love, and perhaps even regret that we'd ever had a brief falling out. Herb was now in spirit form, and he literally was "the Aloha Spirit."

In a strange and beautiful way, his visit was a bestowal of a blessing on my calling – I have been the "The Travel Psychologist" ever since those days at the University of Hawaii.

That I may have accomplished something of distinct and unique value in my career and by co-writing this book is succinctly summed up by the Australian psychologist, Shawn Koller, PhD, in his statement:

"Thanks to Michael Brein... to be the pioneer of this field."

Introduction
Rosemary Ellen Guiley

Travel opens many doorways, and one of them is to the Unknown. Most individuals who set off on a trip or vacation do not expect to encounter something from beyond this world. When they do, amazing changes and transformations take place, even if an experience is scary. Not all strange and paranormal experiences are frightening, however, as many of the stories in this book attest. Some are uplifting, inspiring, and even mind-blowing.

Among the stories are unsettling accounts of ghosts and the dead; visions that happen in moments of crisis; past-life revelations; creepy hauntings; bizarre synchronicities; life-changing spiritual lessons; and reminders that we are not alone in the cosmos.

This book came into being because of a travel synchronicity.

I became acquainted with Michael Brein in the early 1990s when our paths crossed many times at UFO conferences and events. Michael was well-known in ufology, even called an "ambassador" in the field. That connection went dormant after a few years as life took us in different directions. Then, an amazing synchronicity happened. One recent summer, I posted on social media that I was in the Pacific Northwest visiting family – I grew up there – and Michael responded. He was now living in the Pacific Northwest, not far from where I was staying!

We got together and the rest, as they say, is history – a collaboration on a truly unique anthology. The treasure chest of paranormal travel stories that Michael has collected for decades reveals a fascinating side of travel that peeks into the Unknown. The stories are entertaining, illuminating, and even educational, as they may help others understand similar experiences.

This is the first of several volumes that we plan. In this volume, we have assembled 44 stories that touch on a wide variety of phenomena and types of experiences. They are grouped under 10 general themes:

- "Ghosts and Hauntings" features phantoms from sorrowful to scary, as travelers unexpectedly pierce the Veil.

- "Encounters with the Dead" reveals astonishing ways the dead participate in the world of the living.

- "Psychic Breakthroughs" includes spontaneous clairvoyance, clairaudience, and psychic phenomena.

- "Premonitions and Omens" showcases eerie forebodings.

- "Predictions and Fate" concerns fortune-telling-for-a-lark episodes that unexpectedly prove to be true.

- "Déjà Vu and Past Lives" shows how people suddenly are confronted with inklings and knowledge of the past.

- "Magic and Curses" demonstrates the dangers that face the unwary traveler, and the real power of magic.

- "Weird Synchronicities" showcases unusual and astonishing connections of circumstances.

- "Time Slips and Other Mysteries" reveals the interdimensional fluidity of our reality.

- "Mysterious People, Spirits, and Beings" features encounters with unknown presences and beings, some of which are dramatic life-changers.

Some of the stories easily could fit in several categories, for paranormal events are not always just a single phenomenon, but a complicated mix.

At the end of every story, I have supplied a commentary to shed more light on what happened, and why. The commentaries and stories are self-contained, but I have sought to minimize repetition of explanations that fit more than one story. As you will see, sometimes it is difficult, if not impossible, to isolate an explanation. Sometimes there are multiple possibilities, including natural explanations. In many cases, the explanations are mind-expanding – as the travelers themselves discovered.

The stories are credited to the authors; only a few asked for pseudonyms. The stories are true and original, and need no embellishment. They will take you deeper into the Mystery.

GHOSTS AND HAUNTINGS

THE BLOOD-SOAKED MAN
Astrid Stromberg

A man covered in blood limps down a Paris street and then vanishes.

The man was bloody, from head to toe, walking towards me on the famous Rue Sainte Anne. It was 1997, I was in my twenties, working in finance and insurance and sharing a loft apartment with my sister in the heart of Paris, France – the Louvre in one direction and the Palais Royal in the other.

It was a pleasant early evening, perhaps around 5 PM, when I walked my happy little dog, "Giggles," down Rue Sainte Anne. Back in the apartment was my sister, probably making her amazing onion pie while jamming to music.

The Rue Sainte Anne was named after Queen Anne of Austria. It was a little narrow street that once housed politicians, philosophers, and alchemists alike. During the 1900s, the neighborhood declined. On either side, massive oak carriage doors carried you through time as you entered cobbled courtyards to private apartments that were four stories high.

The blood-soaked man of Paris confounds a witness. Credit: John Weaver.

Giggles, tugging at her leash, suddenly stopped. I looked up and saw a man, about five-foot-nine, walking toward me, drenched in blood from head to foot. He looked like he had just been slaughtered! The weird part was that I hadn't seen him coming, despite the straightness of the road and the light of day.

Three feet away, I asked him, "Can I help you, are you okay?"

No response. He just stopped, shook his head, and stared at me.

"What's your name?" I asked.

Then he turned toward my neighbor's massive oak wood carriage door entrance, and walked through it.

Now, this carriage door could only be opened with a digital key: a code on the left of it that let you in. But sometimes, because the doors were so heavy, they didn't always quite lock all the way. As he went through it, I ran to catch it open just in time, but when I looked in the courtyard, he had already disappeared.

You don't encounter bloody people like that in Paris, ever! Perhaps at the cemetery of the "Père Lachaise," where Jim Morrison and Oscar Wilde lie in peace.

I had been down that road countless times, but never had I encountered a man dripping blood from head to foot.

There were a few people walking in the street at the same time as me. But, nobody seemed to take notice. When the man appeared, it was just him and my dog and me on the same side of the street. I remember a couple of other people on the other side, but they didn't stop or even seem to see what I was seeing.

The center of Paris is said to be a hub to ghosts of both world wars and other detrimental events throughout the years. To me, it was a simple validation, that whatever you see may not appear to be what it seems.

I learned afterward that this street had had its lot of political intrigue and that "bad things happened behind those doors." Private hotels holding séances, prostitutes, and even the infamous alchemist Saint Germain himself may have once lived a couple doors down from me.

Why the blood-soaked man? I have no idea. The street was mostly always peaceful.

When I told my sister and asked her what she thought, she just replied that I must have seen a ghost.

I really thought it was a real man – but then how could there have been no blood dripping onto the ground? How could he have disappeared so fast when I was just three feet away? He was limping – and I was fast on his heels as he made for the door. There was no way he couldn't have left blood stains on either the street or the door that he had to have pushed to get through, and there was no way he could have gone anywhere that I wouldn't have seen him go. He just disappeared!

Commentary
Astrid experienced an unusual type of apparition, one that interacted with her. Many ghosts seem real and solid until they mysteriously disappear, as the bloody man did. In most cases, they are residual imprints, a supernatural "recording" that repeats a certain action in the same place. The bloody man may have been fatally wounded when alive, and managed to walk partway down this street in Paris. As Astrid discovered, the center of the city was known for ghosts of World Wars I and II, as well as other times.

Imprints usually vanish into thin air or go through a wall or something solid and then disappear. This ghost, however, opened the carriage door, and without using the digital code key. In the past, these doors had no such modern locks, and he opened them as he might have done so in an earlier time.

The bloody man did not speak, but shook his head when asked if he needed help. Imprints have no awareness and do not interact. So, what exactly was this man?

It is possible that he was an earthbound soul, someone who has not crossed to the afterlife after death, but remains in a twilight realm in the physical world. People become earthbound if they do not realize they are dead. Sometimes they successfully resist their transition because they have unfinished business. Eventually, they do cross over, but they may be stuck for indefinite periods of time until they do.

Perhaps the bloody man was killed in one of the wars. He may have been fatally wounded and covered in blood, and managed to walk down the street in a daze until he collapsed and died. Perhaps he didn't realize he died, or he refused to acknowledge it, and his earthbound condition was created. Astrid did not comment on the man's clothing, but it was modern enough not to look out of place, so we can speculate that he died in World War II.

Earthbounds can look solid or look like ghosts, and they are not perceived by everyone, which explains why Astrid alone saw him.

The bloody man will probably walk the Rue Sainte Anne until he finds the door to the afterlife.

GHOST IN THE BLACKNESS
Vince White

*A man is startled by the scary apparition of a girl while staying in a
medieval village.*

Starting in 1979, I spent a year-and-a-half backpacking throughout Europe. During my travels, I spent some time in Bardou, in the Languedoc-Roussillon region of France, a tiny village in a mountainous area. It was largely in ruins and was being restored, house by house, by a German man who bought and owned the village.

This village had endured plagues during the Middle Ages. And boy, was it dark there! There was no power, no electricity – it was all by candlelight and fireplace. Life was like it had been lived 200 to 300 years earlier. It was very primitive. The village depended on a nearby mountain stream for water.

I rented a 400-year old-house called "The Tower." I slept in a sleeping bag in a loft. I would go to sleep early because of the blackness.

There wasn't a whole lot to do in the dark. I was largely by myself. There were only a few people living in the village – usually no more than four to six people at a time.

One night I blew out the candle, and I had a strange feeling. I looked up and saw this hologram-like cloud of yellow phosphorescent light forming right in front of me. In it shone a little girl with pock marks all over her face and body. She looked sickly and distressed. Then she turned towards me and just stared directly at me, which was quite frightening. There was intelligent conscious energy or consciousness in her. I didn't want to look real close at her eyes, because I was too afraid.

I was pretty rattled and thought, *What do I do? Do I leave this place immediately?* I calmed down and concluded that a ghost was not going to harm me. It was probably someone who had lived there long ago, and now her spirit was here. She had the energy of people who had gone through a time of sickness, like a plague.

I turned away and then I looked back. The glowing girl had just disappeared. Her image simply vanished – it was gone!

I tried to get some sleep. I buried my head in my sleeping bag, hoping that that was the end of it.

The next morning was bright and sunny. The sunshine seemed to dispel what I had seen in the night, so I didn't worry about a thing.

I found out later that two girls had rented and lived in the same tower, and had the same thing happen to them. However, they ran out screaming into the night. They were so horrified and petrified, they would not go back in that house ever again!

I stayed for several months. I wasn't entirely by myself; I had met a nice young Dutch girl, who was bicycling and doing like me, *le vendage* (the gathering in of grapes). We picked grapes to make money during the harvesting season.

I never saw the sickly girl ghost again.

There were some other odd and probably related happenings in Bardou. There were several people who had experiences, leading people to think that this area seemed to be one of great psychic intensity.

For instance, there was a hostel that belonged to the owner of the village. Some people were said to have had some powerful déjà vu experiences when they were there. They seemed to suddenly remember previous incarnations of past lives in this village.

I didn't have any direct memories like that myself, but I still have a strange feeling that I'm going to go back there in the future, maybe in another life. I was practicing writing fiction while I stayed there, and I was spontaneously driven to write a science fiction story about being there a hundred years into the future. I really don't know where that came from. I was compelled in some way to write a fiction story of grapes being picked by robotic overseers, and the way things will be a hundred years on, including getting out of an aerial vehicle of some kind and walking down those same mountain roads as they exist today.

Ever since then, I've tried to understand what the ghost experience was all about. I felt as if the girl's appearance was to communicate a message directly to me. There was an intense psychic connection of some kind between us. I don't know exactly what that was. I just felt that it was personal and meant for me. There was a meaning and a purpose behind her appearance to me, and it wasn't just random.

But sometimes ghosts are said to just be there and not interact and connect with people. In the paranormal literature I've read – for instance, Michael Newton's books on past lives – when people are in the in-between lives state, maybe they dream. Sometimes they dream of physical realities in past lives, and they appear to us in their own dream states, and not in fully conscious states, perhaps just as psychic fragments of themselves, rather than as entire souls. They would look like ghosts to us.

So, maybe there are several kinds of ghosts. Perhaps there are people who die and haunt an area, because they can't connect with the light. There could be people who are in between lives, maybe in spiritual realms, extra-dimensionally visiting past lives and working through their conditions, problems, and challenges by re-experiencing those realities. Who knows?

Here's another aspect of my ghost experience, which has to do with "blackness." It was very intense living in that remote mountain village, because one of the things that people don't appreciate is what "night" really means in modern culture. Artificial light has changed our relationship with the universe.

When it was dark in Bardou, it was really dark – like black dark! The village was in the mountains next to one of the national parks in France, and there was no electricity. A house or two had generators, but where there was no electricity at all, it was truly black. The total darkness made it a very magical place.

To me, the blackness represented rest, recuperation, and soul refreshment. It was not bad, and it did not have a negative connotation at all. Rather, it had a warm, soothing feeling of total rest. One of the things I was told when I got to this village was, "Vince, you move too fast; you think too fast; you need to slow down and find a different rhythm here." After a few weeks, I understood what they meant. I had no radio, no television, no magazines. Sometimes I would hike many kilometers into a neighboring village, where I'd buy *The Economist* or a newspaper just to find out what was going on. And then, I truly appreciated the modern world.

It took the experience of returning to life as it was centuries ago to learn a very valuable lesson about basic survival. You must have your fireplace going when it's cold and wet and damp, and you need to work your fireplace 24 hours a day. Things like that. Fire-tending was a big deal. I finally understood that I had to work very hard to develop a stash of lumber. I was the go-to person – people would come to my house to get their firewood. I was the firewood "sharer."

Another thing, you had to spend hours a day just to cook and clean. You'd spend nearly all your time just dealing with essentials. There was a completely different rhythm and nature to life. It was a totally different focus for me.

I got in tune with a completely different level of myself by being in that environment. It was a formative experience for me. I took for granted, and never really understood, so many things in the modern era, until I'd spent several weeks in that environment far away from radio and television, walking every day and doing a lot of hard physical labor. We need to have more experiences of the total blackness of the darkness of night.

I have no doubt that the blackness contributed to the impact, significance, and meaningfulness of the ghost apparition on that night. It was a truly powerful time.

Commentary

Vince stayed in a small village that was literally out of time, a place conducive to receptivity to the spirit realm, and to having psychic experiences such as déjà vu, past-life flashes, and seeing apparitions. Many old places are full of residual apparitions, which are imprints left in psychic space – the accumulations of long histories of tragedies, plagues, war, and disasters.

The pock-marked girl seems to have been more than an imprint, however, because Vince sensed an intelligent awareness in her. Residual ghosts have no self-awareness or awareness of the living – they simply exist in space just beyond the normal sensory range, and manifest when conditions are right.

The girl may have been an earthbound soul, stuck between life and the afterlife perhaps because of the trauma of her death, which was probably due to plague. Earthbounds sometimes try to get help from the living, but not everyone can see them. They have no sense of the passage of time.

It is not unusual for dramatic apparitions to appear only once or twice. They are dormant until given energy, and the energy may be completely expended in a single appearance. Some appear over and over to the same witness.

No one knows the precise energetic formula that enables a ghost to become visible. The consciousness of the percipient plays a major role. For example, the girl ghost may not have appeared to everyone who stayed at the tower, but only to those who had the "right" energy and receptivity.

Vince's ability to blend in to the rhythm of the village and become absorbed in its lost-in-time twilight undoubtedly was a factor in his experiences, too. He became "tuned in."

THE HOLOCAUST GHOST CHORUS
Michael Brein

A camping experience in Germany turns into an encounter with the dead.

Ever had a paranormal or psychic experience? If you've never believed in the reality of such things as telepathy, ESP, or psychokinesis, it takes only one gripping personal experience to convince you of its reality. It is one thing when it happens to you at home; it's another when it occurs in a foreign country while you are traveling. My Inner Psychic was in tune, aware, and alert one night as I was camped in my VW bus along a riverbank just outside Düsseldorf, Germany.

My routine was to go to bed early, wake up at the crack of dawn, take a short jog, and then drop in for an early shower and morning coffee at the home of a couple of German friends who were living close by.

On this occasion, I was sound asleep, feeling comfortable and safe in my bus. Sometime during the night, I began to *"hear"* what I can only describe as surrealistic or ethereal music – more like chanting, if not singing. It was a chorus of many voices, and it did not seem to be coming from the outside. Neither was it coming, strictly speaking, from inside my head. It was a more like a cacophony or chorus of sad, longing, mourning, and suffering voices. There was a religious feel to the sound. I would describe it as "heavenly," but it could not be that, since so much negative emotion and apparent suffering seemed to be involved.

The chorus was not like anything I'd ever *"heard"* before. It was so unreal. I was struck with how incredibly and profoundly sad and deep this music seemed to be.

Was I having some sort of auditory hallucination? No, I thought, because, as a kid, I did have an auditory hallucination once. In this instance, I knew that my mind did not create it; it was not playing tricks on me; and that the sound was, therefore, external to me.

Furthermore, I thought that in an odd way, it was meant for me personally.

It certainly had its effect on me in the early morning. I arose feeling restless and disturbed by it all. It was very much on my mind from the start of my run along the riverbank.

Suddenly, on my right, I came upon an old cemetery. It was overgrown and unkempt, and obviously had not been tended for a long time. When I took a closer look, I saw that it was an old, abandoned Jewish cemetery. No doubt it had fallen into complete disrepair and neglect a long time ago, perhaps even during the Holocaust.

To this day, I remain convinced that I was meant to hear a chorus of restless and mournful souls among the people who were buried in that cemetery. I know in my heart of hearts that I had a paranormal experience there on that night with those unfortunate souls, who communicated to me their profound restlessness, grief, and despair. Perhaps they simply wanted someone to take notice of them – they wanted to be remembered.

Perhaps others who have ventured near this lonely graveyard have also heard the mournful voices.

Commentary
Ghostly voices are a form of auditory residual haunting, like a psychic sound recording that can be perceived when conditions are right. In the

quiet of the night, Michael – who has had psychic experiences in his past – suddenly tunes in to the subtle vibration of the chorus.

We can only speculate as to the identities of the voices. Were they the souls who were buried there – or were they the residual sounds of mourners crying at graveside as their loved ones were put to earth? Perhaps they were both.

Few cemeteries have phantom choruses. Perhaps one of the purposes behind this haunting of an old Jewish cemetery is to keep alive the reminder of the suffering that happened during the Holocaust.

There is perhaps another purpose as well: The dead do not want to be forgotten. Here was an old cemetery that had been long forgotten. Michael's experience, and his writing of this article, have served to preserve the memory of those "forgotten dead."

ALLEY OF THE GHOSTS
Alicia Mannix

A woman stays at a bed and breakfast whose owners deny that it's haunted – but she knows otherwise.

I went to a centuries-old little village, called Frigiliana, Malaga, which is in the mountains, just minutes from the sea, along the Costa del Sol in Spain. It's a gorgeous mountainous village with white stucco homes climbing the hillsides. I was with a group of artists on an 11-day painting retreat. I was assisting the instructor.

We stayed in a bed and breakfast run by a hilarious British couple. It was quite luxurious with a swimming pool and beautiful terraces overlooking the entire town – just simply gorgeous.

A few days into the workshop, I retired early for the evening, feeling very tired and over-stuffed, as I was every night from eating too much. I was sitting silently in my room, writing in my journal for about half-an-hour or so. At about 11 o'clock or midnight, I was relaxing in bed.

Suddenly, I started to feel the bed vibrating in a way that I had never experienced in my life. It was shaking – the bed was moving! It was shaking so much that I wondered if there was an air-conditioning unit underneath my room.

I then realized that the house was hundreds of years old, and had *no* air-conditioning! The walls were about five feet thick, and you couldn't hear a thing once you shut the door.

Then I thought maybe there had been an earthquake, except that this whole thing was lasting way longer than an earthquake, and nothing else was shaking except the bed. I was scared, so I went into the bathroom, not knowing what else to do. When I came back out, the shaking had stopped.

Oh, my God, I thought. *This place is haunted!* I'd encountered ghosts before in some of the old buildings in medieval European towns.

At breakfast, when the whole group was assembled and drinking coffee and eating, I casually mentioned what had happened and asked the hosts if there were any stories about the house having ghosts.

Their eyes literally bulged out as though I'd suddenly struck a nerve. "Oh, of course not!" they exclaimed. "We haven't heard of any stories around here." They went on and on about it, how they had heard nothing of the sort, ever, about the house. "So, Alicia, there are *no* ghost stories!" It was overkill.

I described the shaking bed incident. They laughed and dismissed it as the funniest story they'd ever heard. Even my workshop leader chimed in with a ridiculous pseudo-scientific explanation that it was pure nonsense. She even tried to write it off as deep heart beating, claiming that had happened to her. The British couple loved that. I knew something was wrong in all this over-reaction, but I let it go.

A bit later, I was talking to one of the other participants in the workshop in a more private setting. I asked him if he had any thoughts about what happened to me, since he seemed to be a sensitive guy who would be open to things like ghosts.

"I have a feeling there are ghosts in the house," he agreed.

I pressed him for an explanation, but he just shrugged and said it was a "vibe" he got. He told me about his uncle who owned an old brownstone in Boston. Every night he would hear ghosts rattling a lock and stomping around in the attic. When anyone went up into the attic to check it out, there was no one there.

This fellow was matter-of-fact about the existence of ghosts, and added, "I think the ghosts here are friendly."

I felt a little relieved, but I was still upset, and that night I slept with my lights on. The bed didn't shake. I decided to let it all go and not talk about it anymore. I became preoccupied with my art and did not think much about it again, until one day when I was painting up on the terrace.

I had noticed that sound in the village carried for quite a distance, and it was often possible to hear conversations in houses that were down the way from the B&B. One afternoon, I became aware of loud speech coming from an American-accented man who apparently was giving a tour of the village. He wore a red polo shirt with the website address of a tour company.

He stopped directly below my terrace and announced that underneath the street was an ancient Muslim burial ground, and that this corner of the village has been considered the ghost headquarters of the whole area!

I literally flipped out and my heart pounded. I said to myself, *Yes! I am not crazy! I am not inventing this story – it is legitimate!*

The man took his tour to the other side of the house, and I crossed to the other side of the terrace to listen to the rest of the story. Lo and behold, right on the other side of the terrace in the alley was the place where people were hung during the Spanish Inquisition!

I was dumbfounded. I ran downstairs to the kitchen and called out to the wife owner of the B&B, "Angela, Angela, please come here. I want to tell you something." I repeated what the tour guide had said.

Angela got very upset. "Oh, don't you listen to that crook – he takes everybody around and makes up stories that have absolutely no basis to them – makes them up right on the spot!" she exclaimed.

"But he said the name of our street means 'cul-de-sac of ghosts,' or 'Alley of the Ghosts,'" I persisted. "This is the Alley of the Ghosts!"

Angela retorted, "Every Spanish village has that or a similar name. It's like 'Main Street' in America. Alicia, this man is so cruel. He has a personal vendetta against us and wants to scare our guests. He's jealous of our success. You shouldn't listen to a word he says."

I could see I wasn't going to get anywhere. But more than ever, I was convinced I experienced a ghost.

I tried to figure out why I was the one who had the experience. I was the only Jewish female in the artists' group. I was on top of a Muslim burial ground... and Jews were hung during the Spanish Inquisition right outside the house. I didn't know if those were legitimate explanations, but I couldn't think of anything else.

I avoided bringing the topic up again during the rest of my stay. It seemed to me that the British couple bought the establishment and then discovered that it was haunted. They were stuck with it. Maybe it scared them, too. They tried to squelch ghost stories because they were afraid it would be bad for business. Anyone who stayed there who reported something unusual just got laughed off.

This happened before ghost-hunting became popular on television. The irony is, today many people would deliberately choose a haunted place to stay – and might even pay extra for the privilege!

Commentary
A shaking bed is a common haunting phenomenon. From a paranormal perspective, it is a sign of an active spirit presence, one that likes to pester and upset people. Variations include the bed shaking back and forth as though seized by giant hands; shaking up and down; vibrating as though machinery is running beneath it; sensations of pounding coming up from the bottom of the mattress; and invisible weights coming down on the bed. Shaking beds occur in benign hauntings such as the place where Alicia stayed – there was no marked negative activity that plagued all the guests. Shaking beds also occur in severe, negative hauntings where the spirit is hostile and malevolent, and in cases of extraterrestrial abductions as well.

Alicia was right in her thinking that the subterranean burial ground and the execution site were contributors to the haunting. These factors are similar to ones found in other haunted locations. Also, old towns and places often accumulate residual energy from past events, especially tragic and traumatic ones, that contribute to hauntings.

It is doubtful that Alicia being Jewish and female were reasons why she was targeted. More likely, she had the right sensitivity to the spirit energy that was present. She might have been that way from childhood. She did acknowledge having other ghost experiences. Highly creative people, such as artists, are more likely to have a heightened sensitivity to the spirit realm. If they are in the right place with the right mix of energies, they become lightning rods for phenomena to happen.

THE GHOST DOG
Susan Wick

A frequent business traveler is visited at night by a phantom dog.

Between 1996 and 2001, I was a staff writer for *Touched by An Angel*, a popular CBS television show. We did the writing and post production in Los Angeles, but the show was shot entirely in Salt Lake City. CBS rented a condominium apartment in downtown Salt Lake City for the writing staff who would travel from Los Angeles during the shooting. It was a fairly new, modern building about five years old. It may have been a hotel at one point. We had a large apartment on a high floor.

My job was more specific than some of the other writers, so I was in the apartment more than anyone else. As I was staying there, I started to notice something after I went to bed. I got the sense that something was coming down the long hall that connected the living room to the master bedroom. It seemed to be a dog – the footsteps of a large, heavy dog – with jingling ID tag chains, just casually trotting down the hall toward the bedroom.

A ghost dog still likes a bed in Salt Lake City. Credit: *John Weaver.*

I would look up but not see anything. I was sure that I was awake. I felt, more than anything, that it was a dog. I couldn't see it or smell it, and I honestly couldn't *hear* the dog tags physically, but it was as though I was hearing them inside my head. I had an overwhelming sense that this was, in fact, a dog.

I wasn't threatened or frightened. I had the feeling the dog belonged there, and in a way, it seemed perfectly normal. I wondered, however, if I was dreaming or else making it up because I was tired.

But it happened repeatedly, a couple of times a week, and it was always the same: I would be trying to get to sleep late at night – usually after midnight – and then I would hear the dog coming down the hall.

After a while, I began to get a sense of what the dog looked like. It was a large, pretty, very well kept silver-blue pit bull. It was very healthy. Again, I didn't "see" it literally, but had an impression of it.

So, the dog would come down to the bedroom door, and then I wouldn't feel it any more, as though it vanished. Then, one night it came into the room! That was creepy! I froze, and then it went away. It did that a few times. A while later, he came down the hall as usual, at his normal trot, stopped at the door, as he usually did, came into the room, and stopped halfway between the door and the bed, as he usually did. This time he crossed over to the bed and put his front paws up on the foot of the bed!

I still couldn't see the dog, but I felt everything about it: its size, the way it looked, the fact that it was just a benevolent dog. I felt the weight of its paws hitting the bed as if, say, a 75-pound dog put its front paws upon the bed and just rested there.

I was startled but not scared, as the dog did not seem to be threatening in any way.

I got used to it, but I never told anybody about it because it was weird.

One day I was back in the writers' room in Los Angeles, hanging out with some writers. I was very tired, because I had just come in from Salt Lake City that morning. I was chatting with one of the writers named Jason, who occasionally would go up to Salt Lake City, too. Most of the writers did.

I said, "God, I am really tired. I didn't get much sleep."

"How come?" Jason asked.

I said, "I don't know. Sometimes it's just a little hard to sleep in the apartment."

Out of the blue he exclaimed, "I know! That dog, right?"

My mouth just fell on the table. I said, "Jason, you know about the *dog*?"

"Yeah, it's that big pit bull, that dog that comes down the hall and gets on the bed."

I said, "Does he get on the bed when you're there?"

"Well, not exactly – he puts his paws on the bed."

We talked about what we experienced. Jason sensed exactly the same things I did and he never literally saw or heard anything, either. To him, it was no big deal, just, whatever.

He was annoyed, though, because the ghost dog kept him up when he was tired. He didn't think it was as strange as I did. I thought it was weird as heck, but he was from Arkansas, where those things apparently are quite normal.

As far as we know, we are the only writers who experienced the ghost dog. I asked a few other writers – there were 10 of us – and then eventually everyone on the staff. Nobody else knew what I was talking about, and I think some of them thought I was crazy.

I didn't know anything about the history of the building or the owners of the condominium, but I wondered if a pit bull dog had passed away there.

Maybe Jason and I were the only two to notice the dog because both of us have had psychic experiences. I've known when some people have died before I've heard the news. Jason is probably much more sensitive than the average person, and is open to stuff like this. I think he's probably had many experiences, and therefore, didn't think that this was unusual.

It is naive to think that the reality that we exist in now is the only one, and that this is the only dimension. There is much we don't know, and that's good and wonderful. We should pay attention to it, because sometimes it pays attention to us.

Commentary
Susan and Jason experienced a residual haunting, also called an imprint. It is energy left behind when a person or animal has died. Imprints do the same things over and over, and certain individuals can pick up on them. They eventually fade over time, like a battery that runs down.

Given the strength and energy of the ghost dog – even though it was not visible – it is possible that such a dog had belonged to an owner of the condominium, and had passed away within a few years prior to the renting by CBS. The repetition was probably a habit of the dog when it was alive: after the owner retired to bed, it would pad down the hall, come into the room, and place its paws on the bed, seeking attention.

Residual phenomena do not possess self-awareness and cognition of the living. The fact that the pattern altered, with the dog coming closer to the bed in stages, is probably due to Susan and Jason becoming more fully aware of it over time. The other writers may not have noticed the dog because they were not psychically tuned to it.

Many pet owners have experienced similar post-mortem phenomena with pets, usually a snippet of a repeated behavior: jumping up on laps, furniture and beds; sounds of walking, barking, chirping, meowing; and so on. The manifestation of imprints may be due in part to the intense emotional bonds between humans and pets, which provides an energy. Most pet imprints fade within a few weeks of the animal's passing, but some can last much longer – as in the Salt Lake City ghost dog.

It is an interesting synchronicity that the ghost dog manifested to writers for a television program about angels!

THE HAUNTED CEMETERY
Ken Friedland

Two young lovers experience spirits and strange goings on in a cemetery.

Getting a fright in a haunted cemetery was the last thing I expected while living in a kibbutz near Haifa, Israel. I had just arrived for a stay of some months. There were people from Europe, America, and elsewhere, who had all converged there. We were all going to be living together.

The kibbutz was up on top of the Carmel Mountains outside of Haifa, way the hell out in the forest, with nothing around it for miles. The fields where we worked were down seven miles away, on the Mediterranean in the lowlands. Adjoining the settlement was a tourist guest house called *Beit Oren*, which means "House of the Pines."

I hadn't been there long when I met a woman from Chicago and her brother, who were staying at the kibbutz. He and I got to be very good friends, and I got to know Hertia, his sister. She was attractive, right around my age.

One warm, balmy night she and I took a walk out of the settlement into the hotel area, which had a recreational area with a tennis court and swimming pool. We kept going. We had no idea where we were, because we had only been there a few days. We kept going deep into the forest, which stretched for miles, until we came to a clearing. We stopped there and started fooling around a bit, and talking and having a good time. I was really getting off on it.

In the middle of this very pleasant experience, we both suddenly had a weird, panicky feeling.

Hertia asked me, "Do you feel that? Do you see that?"

I said, "Yes, what the hell is that?"

We were both scared. We didn't know what was going on. We felt like somebody else was there with us – but we could not see them. Whoever it was, they gave us the distinct feeling that we were not wanted there.

It freaked us out, so we pulled up our pants, got ourselves together, and ran back out of the woods, through the hotel area and into the settlement. We were pale and shaking – very scared at whatever was out there in the woods.

We talked to other people about it, but they could not understand what we had gone through or what it was all about. We didn't have any idea what had happened to us or why, and neither of us had experienced anything like that before.

A couple of days later, I got up the nerve to go back to the clearing in daylight to look around and see what might be going on. I found nothing in particular – just a clearing in the trees. I couldn't get our creepy experience out of my mind.

Several days after that, I was on a work detail in the vicinity of that place. We walked down a trail that was near the clearing. At the end of the trail, I was astonished to find a cemetery. I realized with a chill that Hertia and I had been standing right behind the graves of two men who had recently been shot in Africa! They had died violent, sudden deaths. We had been standing right behind their graves, completely unknowing, for it was impossible to see the cemetery in the pitch dark of night.

This really shook up me and Hertia. We told some of our friends back in the settlement about our discovery, and they got spooked, too.

One night, we all screwed up our courage and decided to go in a group out to the cemetery to see if anything else might happen. Something very, very weird did happen. It wasn't just the two of us this time – it happened to the whole group.

We were standing near the same two graves, which were on the end of the cemetery that was closest to the settlement. We were looking out to the far end of the cemetery, which bordered the forest. Once again, the forest stretched for miles and miles before there was any sign of civilization.

We all froze when we heard a woman laughing out there at the edge of the cemetery. It was a wispy, far away laugh, and everyone heard it at the same time. Was someone out there in the darkness? We all went toward the sound – but no one was in sight.

We searched around a bit and found nothing. We all left scratching our heads, wondering what to do next. We avoided that area from then on. We didn't want to go any deeper into whatever mystery was there.

I found out later that there were stories about the place being haunted since biblical times. The spirit of the prophet Elijah supposedly wandered the hills. There were caves near Carmel where he was said to have stayed during his travels.

Maybe so, but Hertia and I felt that if the cemetery was haunted, it was by the spirits of the men buried in the two graves that we had been near. The most likely candidates for ghosts and hauntings are people who have died sudden, violent deaths. Perhaps we pissed them off with what we were doing on their graves!

Commentary
Many cemeteries are haunted, and by more than the restless dead. This cemetery seems to be one of them. Did Ken and Hertia disturb unhappy souls who had died violently, by standing near their graves and engaging in romantic play? It's plausible, and fits a pattern of other haunted cemeteries containing the graves of those who died tragically.

Some cemeteries also attract nonhuman spirits that haunt the grounds, and they are not always friendly. The most common forms they take are dark blobs and apparitional women in white – even though there is nothing human about them.

Who was the laughing woman? There were coyotes in the area, and sometimes they can sound like people talking or laughing. However, this was not a mix of voices, as a pack of coyotes would sound, but a single voice. A "woman laughing in the woods" has been reported in other cases of mysterious phenomena.

The laughing woman also is reminiscent of a banshee type of spirit, a female death omen figure. Some of them lurk about remote areas; this cemetery was in a remote, forested and mountainous area. Banshees usually wail, cry, or shriek, though eerie laughter would not be out of the realm of possibility.

A wandering ghost of Elijah is not a likely explanation. The residual energy, or imprint, of a Biblical-era personality would be faint in today's times, thousands of years later. Even if active, it would probably not be hostile – or laughing. Nonetheless, the area could indeed have a haunting history that goes way back in time.

THE GHOST OF FLOWERHILL MANOR
Steve Cosgrove

A mischievous ghost teases guests by, among other things, stoking a fire in the fireplace.

This is about a haunted manor in Ireland, which is the absolute perfect place for a haunted house. In 2000, I traveled to Ireland with my 10-year-old daughter. It was my first trip there and was a feeling of homecoming for me, for I'm half German and half Irish.

Ireland is such a beautiful country. It's so green that you know full well why it's called the "Emerald Isle," because it's just so gorgeous. I really enjoyed my time there, and I felt like I made a connection that was ancestral. My grandfather came from Ireland. He ran away from home when he was 12 years old and left everyone behind. He stowed away on a tramp steamer to America. I had no idea where his home had been in Ireland, or where any of the relatives were, so I went there without that compass. I thought I would just go and see what happened.

The Irish are great horse people and I have this connection with horses. I've ridden horses all my life, since I was a kid. My daughter rides as well. We love horses.

We decided to spend a week at the Flowerhill Equestrian Center in the East Galway Hunt area, which is famous for horseback riding and fox hunting. We stayed in a 300-year-old Georgian mansion, a converted bed-and-breakfast, built by a reformed drunk. He sold off all his cows and got horses, and converted his manor and estate into this now-famous, state-of-the-art horseback riding and hunting area.

In the morning, we were served a beautiful breakfast by a woman named Mary. She announced to us, "Well, you know, you do need to realize that occasionally the ghost comes."

I just laughed it off. I thought, *This is great; this is part of the Ireland thing.* Since I'm half Irish, I know full well that the Irish are bunch of BS-ers! I've never seen a ghost, and I didn't think I'd ever see one or be around one, either. But Mary was so matter of fact about it. My daughter, of course, was all ears.

I said, "So, who is this ghost?"

She answered, "There was a huntsman here about a hundred years ago." She gave me his name, and said he was the master of the hounds. He was a notorious drunk. He used to go out in the middle of the night and start drinking, and then he'd run the hounds by the moonlight. He was often out as late as midnight. One night, drunk out of his mind, he was running the hounds and hit a tree head on, which killed him instantly. Ever since, he is said to come back to haunt the manor.

Well, I initially let it go. But two days later my daughter and I, after breakfast, were sitting in front of the fireplace, which they fired with peat, a real slow burning fire. Only the two of us were in the room. All the windows were closed.

All of a sudden, the fire started to stir. I thought it could be just a breeze coming down the chimney, but as I was looking at the fire I saw a poker move from the fireplace and fall to the floor away from where I was sitting. It moved and then fell right to the floor with a loud thud!

My daughter saw it as well. We both looked at each other, and my rational mind was trying to find the explanation for it. I couldn't, for the life of me, figure it out. We weren't in an earthquake zone, and there was no breeze at all. Absolutely nothing was going on. The fire stirred the coals; the embers all of a sudden got a lot brighter, and the fireplace poker moved and fell to the floor.

I told Mary about it.

She said, "Yes, that's the huntsman. He came to stir the fire for you." Again, she was so matter of fact about it.

I didn't know what to think. The Irish love practical jokes, and my guess was – if the place was haunted, and if it was the ghost – he probably had a great sense of humor, probably heard me expressing my disbelief, and showed me, all right!

There was more. We stayed there for 10 days. I heard sounds at night, even a creeping up the stairs. I'd go out of my room to look, and, of course, no one was out there. The first couple nights, I couldn't sleep very well, so I went downstairs. The owner of the manor had told me, "There's a bottle of cognac in the cupboard there. I don't drink anymore; it's here for the guests. Go help yourself."

So, I would go down and sit in this great big Georgian mansion sitting room. The sitting room alone was probably as big as my house. I would hear things. I was tuned in. I have to admit, it changed my mind about the reality of ghosts. I didn't absolutely believe, but now I didn't disbelieve, either.

Commentary

Many old homes have a ghost or two rattling around in them, especially in places such as Ireland, where supernatural lore is strong. The story of the huntsman involves a real person, but his manner of death may be more legend than fact – violent or unusual death is often tied to hauntings.

Steve experienced typical haunting phenomena in the strange sounds and the noise creeping up the stairs at night. Houses, especially old ones, creak and groan with changes in temperature and moisture, so sometimes it is difficult to know what sounds are natural and what might be paranormal. The sounds of something moving up the stairs is a common haunting phenomenon. When a person investigates, the sounds abruptly stop.

Most hauntings are residual; that is, they are like leftover memories of activity that play like a video or audio loop. In this case, however, Steve and his daughter experienced something more unusual that indicated the possible presence of an intelligent, interactive ghost or spirit. The stirring of the fire seemed aimed at getting his attention, even upsetting his applecart, which it accomplished. It was as though a prankster personality wanted to play a joke on a disbeliever. Mary took it all in stride – she had probably seen and heard much more.

Steve makes the comment that he was "tuned in." His ancestral connection to Ireland may have helped to awaken some natural psychic ability – Irish are famous as seers.

Many disbelievers and skeptics change their minds when they have experiences they cannot explain. So it was for Steve.

TERROR IN TOMBSTONE
Christopher Patrick

Did a man become possessed by a ghost in a famous Old West haunted town?

I n 2008, I was working as a tour leader for a group of 12 people on a 21-day trip from Los Angeles to New York City via a southern route. We traveled in a large, extended van, and camped out in tents. After visiting the Grand Canyon, we headed for Tombstone, Arizona, one of the most famous towns of the Wild West. The old, original buildings from the nineteenth century have been preserved, along with the dirt streets.

Tombstone is especially famous for the "Gunfight (or Shootout) at the O.K. Corral," a violent shootout between lawmen (the Earp brothers Wyatt, Morgan, and Virgil, and their associate Doc Holliday) and members of the Clanton-McLaury gang, a loose group of cattle rustlers, thieves, and murderers. The confrontation took place at about

3 PM on Wednesday, October 26, 1881. It lasted about 30 seconds, and 30 shots were fired. Two of the outlaws were killed.

The gunfight did not actually take place in the O.K. Corral, but in a narrow lot on the side of C.S. Fly's Photographic Studio on Fremont Street, six doors west of the O.K. Corral's rear entrance. The event has been immortalized in fiction and film, especially the 1957 film *Gunfight at the O.K. Corral* starring Burt Lancaster as Wyatt Earp and Kirk Douglas as Doc Holliday, and the 1993 film *Tombstone* starring Kurt Russell as Wyatt Earp, Val Kilmer as Doc Holliday, Sam Elliott as Virgil Earp, and Bill Paxton as Morgan Earp.

Tourists love the town because of the Old West trappings and the daily reenactment of the gunfight.

We arrived in town, set up our tents and showered up, and then everybody had some free time to walk around the town before the gunfight.

Afterwards, we had dinner, and I offered to take anyone interested to a couple of bars. I knew that one of the main local character actors in the shootout, "Doc Holliday," was out and about in the town and would likely be in one of the bars. Just like the real Doc Holliday, he was good at cards and with his gun, and was the "go-to guy" for tourists. It would be cool to go hang out with him.

So, we passed through the famous swinging doors of Big Nose Kate's Saloon and, of course, everyone wanted to mosey over to the bar and order a whiskey to experience the whole ambience of old Tombstone.

I occasionally have tourists from around the world, and this time I had a couple of people from Japan. As a rule, the Japanese don't drink much, and these two pretty much stayed that way throughout the night.

We all hung out with "Doc Holliday" for a while, and he was quite entertaining. We also met a couple of other reenactment characters – one who played the bartender, and one who played the deputy sheriff. They were from Minnesota, which is where I am from, so we had an instant connection.

As the night wore on, they said, "Oh, it's getting close to midnight. Would you be interested in going for a walk with us?"

We thought, why not, as it was around the time when the Bird Cage Theatre ghosts are supposed to become active. It sounded tantalizing.

The Bird Cage Theatre is one of the most famous old buildings in Tombstone. During the 1880s, it was renowned as the wildest honky-tonk in the West, serving as a gambling hall and brothel more than as a theater. It was only in operation for eight years before it was shut down. During that time, 20 gunfights and 20 murders occurred there, and you can still see bullet holes in the place. Wyatt Earp, Doc Holliday, and Bat Masterson were some of the famous people who hung out there.

The Bird Cage was best known for its prostitutes, called "soiled doves" and "tainted angels," who entertained their clients in little rooms called cribs on the balcony level while exotic dancers performed downstairs on stage, and cowboys got drunk and gambled. It must have been quite a scene!

The theater is a museum now, and it is said to be full of ghostly phenomena, such as phantom footsteps, smells, and voices; objects moving around; and apparitions of people dressed in period clothing. Paranormal investigators say that something messes with their equipment, draining the batteries and turning lights and cameras on and off.

My passengers' ears perked up on this and were quite interested in visiting the theater when the ghosts are supposed to be the most active.

We all made our way out of the bar and onto the street. Our hosts told us to walk down the middle of the street to avoid detection by the ghosts. If we walked on the boardwalks, the creaking sounds would alert them more.

It sounded odd, but I had been a tour leader for five years, and had witnessed some things I couldn't explain. I'm always open to experiencing something strange, and until there is significant proof that it's not what it's purported to be, or if it seems like a scam or something is not quite right, then I'll withhold judgment.

I was completely open to Bird Cage experiences, and of course, my passengers were excited. We all knew that this was a very special and unusual opportunity. It was not the typical experience offered to tourists. It was all pretty cool.

I didn't know what to expect. I guess my initial expectations were based on what I had seen in movies and TV shows about Tombstone. I was thinking in terms of picture frames with eyes moving from side to side, chandeliers turning on and off, and maybe some cards being played without anybody there, and so on.

Our hosts told us that recently a ghost-hunting TV show had been there. Within 20 minutes, one of the camera guys ran out of the building terrified. I wondered if that was real, or just a story to get me and my group even more excited – and maybe a little scared – in anticipation of trying to find a ghost.

When we got there, we fanned out through the rooms. The place was backlit from the lights of the street. We kept looking, but no one saw any ghost activity.

Our hosts began telling us things that they had experienced, such as orbs and sounds of yelling and screaming. One of them had seen a candlestick on the bar move, and one of the bartenders, who hosts the museum, said that she'd once seen a glass move – it fell to the floor and then it came back up!

We all kept looking for ghosts, but soon it seemed that nothing was going to happen, so we just hung out and talked with our hosts.

Then one of my Japanese clients, who had not been drinking, tugged on my shirt and said, "I'm just going to sit for a while and then head back to the tents."

"Okay," I said. The campground was close by, just 75 yards or so down a nearby dirt road off the main street. He went to sit on a cowboy bench along the street.

Finally, it got late, so I announced, "Okay, it's time to go, we have a long drive tomorrow to San Antonio."

We headed over to the Japanese fellow to fetch him, but found him sitting there motionless. At first, we thought he was sleeping, because he had his head tilted down a little bit, resting his chin to his chest.

I said, "Okay, it's time to go," but he didn't respond. We tugged on him, and suddenly he jolted up. His eyes looked strange – he stared straight ahead without blinking.

I asked, "What's going on?"

He didn't answer but abruptly raised one of his arms and pointed toward the street. He looked like a zombie, with one arm straight out with his finger pointing.

The lady who had invited us to the Bird Cage started taking photos of where he was pointing and where he was *not* pointing. When we looked at the photos, there was a large mass of orbs floating around, like bubbles you make by blowing.

I had seen one and two orbs in photos before, but there were dozens of them! We were all gaga over this. It was the first time many of us had ever experienced anything like this. It seemed surreal, and we were captivated.

I still was concerned about our Japanese man, and I asked him, "Are you okay?"

He just dropped his head again to his chest and his arm to his side. No one had any idea what was going on with him. He was not responsive to us.

After about a 30-second pause, he raised his head up again, but swung one arm to his right at a two o'clock angle pointed at something we could not see. The lady took more photos. No orbs showed up – apparently, they had moved on in another direction.

Some of my group started to get scared. This was getting creepy, like something supernatural was going on. We wondered if we should lift our man up and carry him, or try to wake him up.

One of the men and I decided to lift him up, and we threw our shoulders under his armpits, pinned his arms around our necks, and lifted. He was a small guy, around 110 pounds, so it should have been easy. I'm 5 feet 11 inches tall and 175 pounds, and the other guy was even bigger than me, but we couldn't dead lift him! It was like he weighed a ton!

That clinched it for me that something supernatural was going on.

The lady said, "I think this sort of thing has happened before. One of the spirits inside the Bird Cage is in him right now and has possessed him! What's to come, I just don't know. Sometimes, there is really a good ghost; sometimes there are really nasty ones."

I didn't react to this – it's my job to remain calm no matter what happens, so that people don't panic. I figured that unless heads started spinning and fireballs started coming at me, there was nothing to get alarmed about. The lady gave me a sense that this was not a worst-case scenario.

We tried to lift him again, without success. Since he wasn't responding to English – even though he was fluent in it – I asked the other Japanese client to try speaking to him in Japanese. He made no response to that, either.

One of the girls in our group started to cry. The lady who took the orb photos said, "It's in him right now, but they generally won't stay around for very long."

Suddenly, his shoulders relaxed and his chin fell to his chest. He popped up his head, looked left and right, and then directly at us. He seemed to be fully conscious.

We huddled around him, overjoyed and relieved that whatever was affecting him was gone. He seemed surprised, and said, "Wow, why is everyone looking at me? What do you guys want? What did I do?" He was completely shocked.

We hugged him and told him the whole story. He had been oblivious to it all, and did not recollect a thing or experience any of the possession.

Now, I must acknowledge that this man was an actor in his student life, and some people in our group thought that maybe this was one of his acting gigs. He was a sweet, kind, and considerate guy, and I don't think it would have been in his nature to pull a trick on us. Nonetheless, I pulled him aside the next day when we were alone, and said, "You know, you have a lot of people really shaken up and frightened, so it's probably best if you fess up now. If this is a joke, you win an Academy Award! You really fooled us!"

He looked at me and said, "No, I don't remember what happened. I just remember feeling a little tired and walking over to the bench, and that's the last thing I remember."

Of course, I took his word for it, and I led the rest of the trip back to New York without further incident.

Our Japanese man ended up studying in Wisconsin, which is where I went for a while with my family. I attended one of his plays once, and he was just great. I don't think he knew at all how to play the role of being possessed by a ghost. But now he certainly does, since we jogged his memory!

When I retell this story, it probably causes a lot of people to think about the spiritual or supernatural world, because this story has the evidence of having so many people witness and experience it – so I think there's a lot of weight to it – and I don't try to fluff up the story at all. It is what it is, you know! The pointing to the orbs; the dead weight that we couldn't lift; how he came to after the spirit had left him – it definitely changed my perspective on these sorts of things. I had already been open to the possibility of ghosts and spirits – but this one really seals the deal.

I don't know how the Japanese man was affected by his experience. He never mentioned anything about it being life-changing, or that he started sleeping with one eye open. But I am left with these thoughts: Why was he the one who went out to the bench? Was someone or something summoning him? Was he selected as the best candidate, perhaps the least jaded, the most open, and the least knowledgeable of any these things, and, therefore, the best person to be lured out to that environment where the possession took place?

Lots of interesting questions remain.

Commentary

Tombstone, Arizona is famous for its ghosts as well as its place in the history of the Wild West. The Bird Cage Theatre is one of the most haunted of all the old buildings, and is a favorite of paranormal investigators. Some of them who perform on television exaggerate by overreacting and running around screaming or acting terrified.

Most of the haunting activity in Tombstone is residual, that is, a collection of imprints with no self-awareness. Such activity comprises footsteps, smells, breezes, voices, odd noises, apparitions, and so on. Residual phenomena are most likely to be noticed when an environment is quiet, such as late at night, but they can occur during the daytime as well.

It is possible that earthbound spirits of the dead, plus nonhuman spirits who masquerade as the dead, reside in the phantom zones of the Tombstone buildings and town. These entities might account for the movement of objects, interactions with visitors, and even perhaps temporary possession.

In a possession, a spirit invades a person and exerts varying degrees of influence. The most common are emotional and mental, in which a person feels controlled or manipulated by an unseen voice or presence. A full possession occurs when a spirit takes over physically and affects a person's body. Those possessions are much less common than emotional and mental ones, and when they occur, they usually do not end of their own accord, but require exorcisms.

It is difficult to assess whether the Japanese man was indeed physically possessed, or was temporarily affected – or "possessed" – in other ways. The lack of reaction, staring at something invisible to others, weird body movements, and inexplicable heaviness are signs of physical possession – but conversely, those symptoms do not mean that a person is physically possessed. Assuming the man was under the influence of some spirit, human or otherwise, he was more likely in a temporary, afflicted trance.

Perhaps he was tired and fell asleep on the bench. Spirit invasion can occur during sleep, so perhaps this type of influence did take place. We have the testimony of the woman taking photographs that this sort of thing had happened to others before. She said it was caused by spirits inside the Bird Cage – but this occurred beyond the theater, outside on the street.

A possible natural explanation is the man experienced a form of sleepwalking. Perhaps he fell into a deep sleep and then seemed to come awake while he was still asleep. Sleepwalking episodes include various body movements and even walking about. The eyes are wide open in a stare. Sleepwalkers usually are nonresponsive to verbal communication. We do not know, however, if this man was prone to sleepwalking.

People who are asleep or in a trance state are harder to lift than people who are awake. This is a natural phenomenon, not a supernatural one. A conscious person who is being lifted shifts body mass automatically to assist the lift. A person who is asleep or in trance is literally a "dead weight" because of the way the body mass is distributed.

As for the orbs, it is impossible to say whether they were a supernatural phenomenon. Everyone had been walking on dirt streets. Fine dust particles kicked up into the air can remain suspended for a long time, and may not be visible to the naked eye. They would appear as masses of fuzzy dots in photographs.

As Chris notes at the end of his story, there are indeed unanswered questions. We can certainly say that an odd, possibly paranormal, event occurred in a famous haunted town.

Some final notes: The fact that the group went looking for ghosts inside the Bird Cage Theatre and experienced no activity is a common experience, as most paranormal investigators discover. When it comes to the paranormal, the more you hunt for it, sometimes the less likely you are to find it.

The warning to walk down the middle of the street to avoid detection by ghosts sounds like something cooked up for the entertainment of tourists. However, there are many strange and old folklore customs for avoiding ghosts – including wearing your clothing inside out so the ghosts won't "recognize" you.

DINING GHOSTS AND OTHER STRANGENESS
Kim Williams

A woman sees ghosts in a restaurant and has other "freaky" feelings in a mountain resort town.

I'll tell you about my weird experiences in Big Bear Lake, California, which is a mountain ski resort community and summer sports mecca – hiking and mountain biking, and so on. It's located in the San Bernardino Mountains, about 100 miles from Los Angeles. I've been going there for 15 to 20 years. There are a lot of stories about that whole area being haunted.

There used to be a restaurant in town called the Iron Squirrel. It's closed now. I had an experience in the Iron Squirrel one day while I was there eating a meal with friends. I happened to look over to a corner, and I saw a group of people at a table. They were older people dressed in older styles of clothing, like turn of the century. I didn't notice if they were eating, but I sure did notice *them*, because they looked really out of place. Then I turned to talk to the people I was with, and when I looked back over to the corner, they were gone! Vanished! I was confused.

I'm not one who usually sees ghosts, but I do experience the energies of a place. I've had paranormal activity since I was little, but I rarely see a ghost that looks like a person.

I talked to the waitress about it, and she said, "Oh, yeah, people like that walk in and out of here all the time, and sit down at the tables." She said that it was almost a daily occurrence in that restaurant for her. I think she was okay with it.

As I mentioned, I am sensitive to the energies in places, and I had strong reactions to some other places in Big Bear Lake. The original theater is now a movie theater. I saw a couple of movies there. It seemed that the feelings I experienced were way more intense than warranted by the movies, especially scary ones. I felt like I was going to freak out. It was like the building was magnifying things.

Another place was the Knickerbocker Mansion, where me and my family stayed in 1996. We had the guest house at the mansion, which was like a suite. I found the energy there to be so intense that I had a hard time with it. I did not sleep. It was freaky energy that made the hair stand up on the back of my neck. I had to leave the room my husband was in and go sleep in the room with my kids.

We stayed there two nights. I felt I had to get out, because there was no rest for me. I felt cold breezes even though all the windows were shut. I heard there was ghost activity in the main house and guest house, too. When we finally left, I felt incredible relief.

Commentary
Many people who take vacations find out their destinations come with a few "extras" that are not of this world. Residual ghosts in hotels and restaurants are common, especially if the establishments have been in business for a long time. Residual ghosts are imprints, recordings of the past. They are always seen in the same places, doing the same things, and they are usually oblivious of the living. They vanish suddenly. They are harmless.

Employees of places haunted by residual ghosts either get used to the activity, as Kim's waitress did, or, if unnerved, leave. Not all staff will experience the ghosts, by sight or sound. Some individuals are "tuned in" to the spirit world more than others. Everyone has a different threshold when it comes to the paranormal. Thus, you can ask several employees about the presence of ghosts and get different responses from each one, from denial to frequent sightings. In addition, what upsets and scares one person will not bother another.

Big Bear Lake has its share of haunting phenomena, and has attracted paranormal investigators over the years. The Knickerbocker Mansion was named after Bill Knickerbocker, a key figure who settled in the region in the early twentieth century. The operators of the mansion make no claim to the place being haunted. Ghosts have been reported on land in the area once owned by Knickerbocker.

Kim's sensitivity to the "energy" she felt in different places is a common phenomenon, too. There are several possible explanations:

- She picked up on residual hauntings that manifested – for her – only as unsettling feelings.

- She unwittingly spooked herself, knowing that the resort community had ghost activity.

- She picked up on earth energy that had an unsettling effect on her. Natural magnetic anomalies and other geological characteristics have real psychophysical effects on some people. Depending on the anomaly, the earth energy can be upsetting or pleasing. The San Bernardino Mountains were formed by fault blocks, of which the Big Bear block is one. The mountains run alongside the massive San Andreas Fault. The area is prone to earthquakes, and even minor tremors will release energy into the landscape.

In addition, some people are sensitive to high elevations. The elevation of Big Bear Lake is 6,752 feet.

Perhaps Kim's experiences were combinations of all these factors. They illustrate how individuals can find themselves in unexpected circumstances, perceiving a reality that is not always evident to others.

THE GETTYSBURG GHOST KIDS
Rosemary Ellen Guiley

Ghostly residents from a Civil War battle make a startling appearance.

Ghosthunting is one of my favorite activities, and I am always interested in haunted places when I travel. Sometimes nothing happens, and sometimes you get a surprise. My visit to Baladerry Inn in Gettysburg, Pennsylvania delivered quite a suprise.

Gettysburg was the scene of the most important battle of the American Civil War, which took place July 1-3, 1863. Up until then, the Confederacy was gaining the advantage. The battle, a horrific, violent shedding of blood, turned the tide for the Union. For three hellish days, the sleepy little town of Gettysburg and the surrounding farm countryside were under a siege of bullets and cannonades as North and South clashed. When the fighting was over, there were between 46,000 and 51,000 casualties of dead and wounded. Thousands of dead horses were strewn all over the enormous battlefield. The homes and buildings in town were riddled with bullet and mortar holes. It took many months to clear the death and wreckage.

Gettysburg draws millions of visitors every year, among them many people who hope to encounter ghosts. The place is famous for residual imprints. Many people have experiences on the battlefield, and just about every hotel, inn, and bed and breakfast has a ghost or several rattling around.

During the battle, most of the farms in the area were pressed into service as field hospitals or officers' quarters. Their wooden floors still have bloodstains from the many amputations of limbs that took place. The lead bullets shattered bones, and sometimes the only life-saving option was to cut off a limb – often without the benefit of chloroform.

In 2004 I joined up with a group of paranormal enthusiasts and we stayed a weekend at the Baladerry Inn, a lovely bed and breakfast located just outside the boundary of the Gettysburg National Military Park, which encompasses the battlefield. The oldest section of the inn was built in 1812 on the Bushman Farm. An addition in 1830 completed the main house. It was originally a tenant farmer's home, and during the war it was used as a field hospital for the Army of the Potomac, the principal Union Army under the command of George B. McClellan, Ambrose Burnside, Joseph Hooker, and George G. Meade. Today the B&B consists of the main house and a carriage house. And yes, the dining room has bloodstains from being turned into an operating theater during and after the battle.

I was given a room in the front of the carriage house on the main floor. There were also rooms upstairs. Every room in the inn, including the carriage house, was occupied by our group.

On the first night, I retired sometime after midnight. I was awakened in the middle of the night by loud scraping sounds above me. It sounded like someone was dragging a large, heavy object, like a crate or chest, slowly across the floor. I looked at the clock, and saw the time was 3:15 AM. The scraping went back and forth, back and forth. I knew there were a couple of guys from the group right above me, and I assumed them to be the cause of the racket.

Ghost girl and boy manifest at the Baladerry Inn, Gettysburg, Pennsylvania. Credit: RE Guiley.

For God's sakes, I thought. *What are those guys doing up there, that they have to do it in the bloody middle of the night?* I was annoyed that my sleep was disrupted.

At last the sounds subsided and I went back to sleep.

The next morning at breakfast, I saw the occupants of the room. "What on earth were you doing last night?" I asked. "It sounded like you were moving the furniture around."

They looked at each other and then at me. "That wasn't us," one said. "We heard it, too, and we thought it was *you* making all that noise!"

Upon further inquiry, it turned out that everyone staying in the carriage house had been awakened by the same noise, and blamed it on someone else.

The loud scraping sounds repeated the second night, at about the same time. Yet nothing was ever physically moved.

Another phenomenon I experienced in my room was tapping on the walls at night. It sounded like someone lightly rapping their knuckles on the wall. The rapping sound would go around the walls for about a minute or two and then stop.

But the best of all was the most amazing ghost photograph I have ever captured.

Ghostly images often show up on reflective surfaces like windows and television sets that are turned off. Such images sometimes register on photographs even though they are not seen by the naked eye. When I visit a haunted location, I take scores of random photographs to see if anything will show up.

On my last day at the Baladerry, I took another round of random digital photographs of the grounds, buildings, and rooms. I went outside the carriage house and photographed the windows and the sliding glass door of my room. No one was inside.

When I examined the photos later, I literally got an electric shock when I saw the one I had taken of the sliding glass door of my room. There in the glass were two images, a female and male, both dressed in period clothing. The male looked like a boy. I could see his facial features and right arm that appeared to be hugging a box or possibly a small piece of luggage against his body. The female figure, slightly taller, looked like a girl. She had a bonnet on her head, and I could see her facial features as well. The lower portions of their forms were incomplete.

There were long drapes on the inside of the sliding glass door, and one panel was pulled a bit to the side by a tie in the middle. The drapes were partially obscured by the figures.

I examined the photo carefully and had other experts examine it as well. There was no way that random reflections could account for the images. They were not vague shapes, but had distinct details.

Who had I captured? The images of people who had lived there, perhaps at the time of the battle? They looked like children – perhaps they were brother and sister. Were they the ones tapping the walls in my room? I will never know the answers. But it's still the most amazing unexplained photograph I have taken, in all the many haunted places I have visited.

Commentary
The Gettysburg town, environs, and battlefield area are full of residual haunting phenomena. Residents and visitors often encounter apparitions and phantom sounds and smells.

Some of the other guests that weekend at the Baladerry had experiences as well, both onsite and on the battlefield. Misty, vague shapes were seen floating on the grounds at night, and odd sounds were experienced inside the main house.

The ghost-in-a-window phenomenon is frequently reported. Sometimes people look in a window and see "someone" looking back; or, like me, they take a photograph of a what appears to be a blank window and find that something shows up in the photograph.

Why do ghostly images appear so often on reflective surfaces? We have no good answers for how ghosts manage to manifest, but reflective surfaces seem to be ideal canvases. Backgrounds, such as foliage, also provide good canvases. Skeptics are quick to argue that the images are random patterns on natural backgrounds, and the eye sees what it wants to see – a natural phenomenon called pareidolia. That may indeed be the case for some vague images that are hard to distinguish, but it is not an adequate explanation for detailed forms.

Ghostly images of people are seldom full-figured. Most commonly, the upper portions of the body are seen and the lower portions trail away and are not visible or incomplete. Details of hands, lower limbs, and feet are usually not captured in a photo.

My ghost photograph was too clear for the pareidolia argument. Nonetheless, the photo becomes a piece of evidence only in support of ghosts, not proof of ghosts.

The scraping sounds in the middle of the night also are a common phenomenon of hauntings. The noises always sound like someone dragging heavy furniture, like a chest or an armoire, across a wooden floor. Upon inspection, there either is no furniture, or all pieces are in their places. Sometimes the sounds stop as soon as a person approaches a room or opens the door to investigate. Why spirits like to imitate scraping furniture noises is another mystery. Perhaps it is an easy sound to make – or, the spirits like to do things that annoy and confound people. Wall tapping also is common, and the same explanations may apply.

As for the ghostly boy and girl: Gettysburg has many ghostly residents, most of whose names will never be discovered.

ENCOUNTERS WITH THE DEAD

WRATH OF THE DEAD
Greg Strickland

*The apparition of a dead woman emerges from her jungle grave
and destroys something that offends her.*

This is a story about the return of the angry dead that I witnessed in Papua New Guinea. I was living in Yakoi Village on the northeast coast of New Guinea, in a hut with a native family. This area of New Guinea was known for a cult of ancestor worship. They placed a great deal of emphasis on their relationships with the spirits of their dead relatives.

I was living with a man named Willie Umbo and his family. Willie liked to tell me how he could make contact with his dead father and mother.

He had a small problem. His stepbrother was building this house for his wife and kids, right in the place where Willie's mother used to spend her afternoons sitting in a rocking chair. She used to build a little fire there and sit and rock and think and whatever. I had known his mother, for she was still alive the first year that I lived with the family. She treated me like a son, and we were quite close.

Willie told his stepbrother, "Listen, I don't want you to build a house here, because it will upset mother and she won't like it."

The stepbrother said, "Aw, that's cool. I don't care about that. I don't believe it." He kept building the house, and Willie decided not to worry about it.

I came down with a bad case of malaria. One evening, I was pretty sick. I had a high fever and my head seemed to be spinning around. I had a feeling that I was going to die. I was lying there half asleep, and I could hear Willie and his family talking about me. They were saying, "All right, we think Greg might… it seems like he almost wants to die."

I thought, *Oh, they're talking about* me. *I better pull myself out of this.*

That night I rallied a bit and forced myself to get up. Later that night a big, strong storm hit. The wind was blowing hard and coconuts were flying, and all kinds of things were going on. Late in the evening it all settled down. I sat up and chatted with the family, out on a little veranda outside of the hut.

Willie suddenly started talking about his mother. He said that he'd been so worried about me and how sick I was, and he'd had this feeling that his mother was going to come and visit, because she was worried about me, too.

Then Willie said, "I can see mother coming! Here comes mother!" He indicated that she was coming down the path from the jungle where she was buried in a graveyard.

Then this wind came up out of nowhere. It had gotten still after the storm, and now a wind was blowing, not strongly, though.

I peered into the darkness but I couldn't see anything. Willie could, however, and he kept describing what his mother was doing, clear as if she was still living. She came walking down the path, straight over to the framework of this little house.

Willie said excitedly, "She's going to wreck the house! She's mad because the house is in her spot!"

I still couldn't see anything, but I started to feel an incredible vibration, as if it was coming from everyone, including Willie. I kept staring at the house, trying to see his mother. All of a sudden, the whole framework of the house just flipped over and smashed to the ground. Just totally wiped out. For no reason! The wind wasn't strong enough to blow it over.

All I could say was, "Wow!"

"Momma just wrecked the house," Willie said. "I told my stepbrother not to build it there. She's really mad now."

Then his mother left.

I never felt her or saw her come near me, even though Willie said she was coming to visit me. By the time she arrived, I was up. I guess she thought that I was okay. She saw the house framework on her spot, got mad and tipped it over and wrecked it.

The stepbrother never built it again. He wouldn't. He believed.

A house is destroyed by an angry dead woman in Papua New Guinea. Credit: John Weaver.

Commentary

Maintaining close ties to the ancestral dead is important in many cultures. In Papua New Guinea, religious beliefs are a mixture of ancestor worship and animism, the belief that everything – people, animals, places, and objects – possesses an indwelling spirit. In more urban areas, Christianity is part of the mix.

In the local tradition where Greg was living, seeing and conversing with the dead would have been cultivated. There also would have been practices of honoring the dead, including not doing things that would make the dead angry. Willie's stepbrother violated that taboo by starting to build a house on a spot that was personally sacred to the mother. No one would be surprised that her riled up spirit would come and knock it down.

Greg's life-threatening illness also played a role in making the visitation possible – there was an urgent need for the ministrations of the dead, who would be believed to hold healing powers.

The storm added physical energy. Wind, rain, and lightning ionize the air. In the buildup before a storm, the air fills with positive ions, which have a "heavy" and "oppressive" feel. These atmospheric conditions are associated with the manifestation of paranormal phenomena.

All the factors created a "perfect storm" for the gates of the underworld to open, and mother to visit and make her disapproval clear.

That Willie saw his dead mother and Greg did not is not unusual in such cases. Willie possessed a greater skill of psychic sensitivity, including clairvoyance. Nonetheless, Greg witnessed the all-too-real effects of the mother's wrath.

THE HELPFUL OLD MAN
Pam Taylor

On a visit to a historical Native American site, two women are aided by a talking ghost.

One of my best friends and I often take a girls' trip out to the desert every year, and we leave all the guys at home, because they don't like the backpacking and the heat. So, a lot of times it's just us girls who go camping.

In 2003, one of my friends and I decided to go to the Four Corners area in southeastern Utah, to a place called Hovenweep National Monument, where Indians once lived in big pueblos with ceremonial kivas. They left their pueblos in the late thirteenth century after suffering a 23-year drought, and migrated south.

The energy at Hovenweep is fantastic. A year or two earlier, we'd had an opportunity to go into one of the areas under excavation and look into a kiva. We like the energy of the area, and the history of it. We also like the geography, and that there is life coming back to that part of the desert. When we go out there and camp, we soak up the atmosphere and enjoy it.

On our way to Hovenweep, we saw a little restaurant and stopped, because we needed gas and food. A nice little white-haired gentleman came out and asked if we needed gas. He wore a gray jacket and had twinkly, clear blue eyes.

We said yeah, and we would go inside and get some food, too.

He said that he would pump the gas for us in the meantime. We thought that was odd, because in Utah most all the gas stations are self-serve, but we didn't say anything.

The place had a lot of hummingbird feeders and we commented on how much we liked them. I had never seen so many hummingbirds, and I started taking pictures of them. He asked if I enjoyed the birds. I said we thought the place was kind of magical.

We went inside, and when we got done eating, we told the proprietors about how nice it was that the kindly old gentleman had pumped our gas for us. They told us no such person existed!

We then went outside, and, indeed, our rental car was full of gas. It had been pumped, and it did show the amount on the gas pump. While we were scratching our heads, a couple of people in the parking lot said they thought the old man might be the former proprietor, who had long since passed over.

We paid for the gas and our food, and chalked it up to being just one of those unique experiences. We went on about our trip.

To this day, I think it was very mystical, magical, and very spiritual. I understand the symbols of hummingbirds and I understand what it is to see somebody in the physical who might not be visible to others.

Commentary
Most ghosts are residues or imprints that do not interact with the living. However, other ghosts that do talk, interact, and perform physical feats have been part of folklore since ancient times. Modern researchers, including parapsychologists, have diverse explanations for ghosts, and divided opinions over whether they can interact with the living. Regardless of where the truth lies, people encounter such ghosts, who

at first seem to be real, solid, living people. The shock comes when the "person" disappears, or the percipient is told that the "person" is dead.

Pam's experience is unusual because it combines several elements that are rarely present together: seeing the ghost in a solid, natural form; conversing with the ghost; and witnessing a physical feat performed by the ghost – filling up the gas tank. Ghosts in haunted locations are often associated with the unexplained movements of objects, but rarely does a witness see the movement taking place.

Another plausible paranormal explanation is that the old man was an angel, one of the "mysterious strangers" who come to the aid of people. Mysterious stranger angels look, talk, and act like living people, and perform physical tasks. When they are done, they disappear. They are often described as having unusual, clear, and sometimes twinkling blue eyes.

Hummingbirds symbolize joy and playfulness, and the enjoyment of life, giving an added meaning to Pam's experience. Perhaps the old man – ghost or angel – and the hummingbirds provided a message to enjoy life while one still has life.

MAN ON DECK
Jess Dropulick

A young woman sees a man who is invisible to another person.
The man's identity is a shock.

In 2004, I was overseas in the military. I was in Iraq for a year, and after that I returned to Germany. But I spent a lifetime, it seems, working with other people in the military service. I learned that you can never understand people, the way they act or the way they think, until you go into a certain situation and you become inundated with the psychic energy surrounding them. It really makes you open up parts of you that you didn't even know you had. So, I guess when I turned 22, I really turned an older age. Does that make sense? I think this is relevant to my story.

The first time I ever saw a spirit was when I had gone to Fort Collins, Colorado in 2005, and then traveled on to Colorado Springs. I had just gotten done with a two-hour massage, and the day before that I had had acupuncture done on my feet and hands.

As soon as the massage was finished, I went to stand in the kitchen of the massage therapist's house. When he went to shut the door, I was looking out and I saw this person standing on the deck outside. I looked at my massage therapist and said, "Did you know you have a person out there?"

He said, "There's no one out there."

I said, "Yeah, I saw somebody! I really did!"

I then described him – his weight, how tall he was, and his hair. The guy looked as if he was probably around 62, balding on top, and heavy-set. He was wearing a plaid polyester button-up, short-sleeved shirt. We made eye contact. The guy looked unhappy. I intuitively knew that he didn't have good energy about him. When he saw me, I'm sure he saw me see him. Then he was gone.

I explained exactly what I saw to the massage therapist.

He replied, "That's my dad, and he's been dead for five years!"

It was weird that I was picking up on *his* energy in *his* house. I said to myself, *Right. Well, there you go. There is your validation!*

It freaked me out. I left to go the Manitou Springs, near Colorado Springs. On the way there, I instinctively put my palm up to where my third eye was and kept waving it in front of my forehead. I felt a beam of energy about the size of a 50-cent piece hit me like a light saber, if you will – just total tangible energy. I don't remember getting from point A to Point B, because I was gone with this whole thing.

Later I found out this guy I had seen on the deck had seven kids. My massage therapist was the last of the seven. The father never treated that child very well, so for some reason his energy was just hanging around his place.

Commentary
It is not unusual for a dead person to be visible to one person and not another, for people have varying degrees of psychic sensitivity. Jess indicates that she had paid attention to psychic impressions in the past. Furthermore, she'd had body work done – acupuncture and massage – which often stimulates the psychic faculty.

The degree of detail she perceived is unusual. Impressions of ghosts and the dead are usually fleeting, and people grasp general features without detail. Her specific description enabled a positive identification.

One explanation for the presence of the dead father is that he was earthbound out of remorse and/or guilt over his treatment of his son, and wished to make amends. His presence seemed to be more like an earthbound than a residual imprint, for Jess felt an intelligent eye contact, which would not have been the case with an imprint. The son either was oblivious to his father or did not want to acknowledge him. Many massage therapists have a keen psychic sense, so he may have been aware of his father at other times. He did not offer an explanation.

For Jess, the encounter may have had a two-fold purpose. One was to validate her psychic ability. Afterwards, she even felt it as a tangible beam of energy coming from her third eye, a chakra point that is between the brows and is the seat of psychic sensing. The second was to make the massage therapist aware of the presence of his dead father. Sometimes people play the role of messenger, and that may have been a purpose here.

A BLESSING IN DISGUISE
Teresa Bright

Visions of the dead appear to a young novice sailor during a critical moment on a rough sea.

In December of 1997, I had a chance to cross the Atlantic Ocean on a sailboat in the ARC, the Atlantic Rally Crossing. There were 200 international sailboats doing the crossing at the same time. I had very little sailing experience, only on the Columbia River and one ocean trip on a sailboat for a few days down the coast of the Baja. That was about it. I wanted to do this trip because I'd always thought it would be really cool to be able to say that I had crossed an ocean on a sailboat.

The opportunity came up with my friends, who were looking for help. They didn't want to cross the Atlantic, just the two of them, so I volunteered. I had the time and the wherewithal to do it. I flew to the Canary Islands and jumped on their 47-foot catamaran. There were the captain and his partner, Wendy; myself; and a retired Swedish naval captain, whom I'd met once before, and who had a lot of good sailing experience on the ocean.

The rally started and we headed out to sea. We were making our way west to the Caribbean, heading to St. Lucia. We crossed over the shelf that surrounds the Canary Islands and headed into deep water. The bar where the deep water meets the shallow water creates steep waves that are close together. We hit this at night, and it was a little scary.

We needed to change the sail from the port side of the boat, the left side, over to the starboard side, the right side of the boat. I wasn't sure what to do, but thankfully, the others did. The wind was blowing and we were heading into the wind. The sails went slack and were flapping noisily. There was so much wind against us, and with so much going on, I was a little bit frightened. It was my first day and night on the boat and I wasn't sure what to do, so I wasn't helping much. I wasn't scared for my life – I was more excited.

I was standing in the sliding glass doorway of the cockpit watching the three of them maneuver to turn the boat and turn the sail from the port side to the starboard side. I was wondering how I could be helpful. Mainly I was trying to stay out of the way. I kept standing there, tethered to the boat with my life jacket on, hanging on, looking out of the back of the boat towards the open ocean in the dark. I was surrounded by loud noises – huge sails flapping around – and we were bobbing around on the ocean like a cork being thrown around.

Suddenly, as if out of nowhere, right above my head and in front of me, appeared the image of my mother, who was deceased. I thought, *Wow, what the heck!* Not only that, within a second or two there was also the face of my dad, who was deceased as well. And just to make matters weirder, right behind him and to his right appeared the face of my brother, who had passed away the year before.

I had eye contact with them. They were facing the others but were clearly looking at me.

My reaction was, *Oh, my gosh!* It happened over a matter of seconds. I was pretty darned stunned by this. My first thought was not to be afraid. I felt they were coming to say as a blessing, "You're doing the right thing. You're in the right place. And we're proud of you." That was what it was – like a blessing to me.

It took about 20 minutes to get the maneuver done, and then we seemed to be fine.

I didn't know the people on the boat all that well, so I didn't tell them what I had seen.

I thought about it more later. I could have been frightened under the circumstances, but my family was there to reassure me that I was in the right place doing the right thing.

I've never had an experience like that again.

Commentary
Spontaneous psychic experiences happen at tense, dangerous moments. In this case, Teresa was frightened but not yet terrified – she may have been too much of a novice to realize the full gravity of the moment. The breakthrough visions of her deceased family members happened at just the right moment to calm her nerves and reassure her that she was in the right place doing the right thing – in other words, all would be well. The eye contact was particularly significant for her, reinforcing the feeling that they were truly there with her in spirit.

Did her parents and brother really appear from the Other Side – or were they hallucinations, symbols of safety and security spontaneously brought up by Teresa's subconscious in a moment of stress? Skeptics might argue for the latter. However, the literature of afterlife visitations includes many such experiences, contributing to a large body of anecdotal evidence that it is indeed possible for the dead to appear in both waking consciousness and dreams.

Some people feel that their dead family members become their guardian angels and will protect them and look out for them. Teresa's family certainly filled that role that stormy night at sea, giving her a blessing she will never forget.

PSYCHIC BREAKTHROUGHS

THE VOICE IN THE STORM
Albert Holdman

A man is twice saved from a potentially fatal accident
by a mysterious voice.

This happened in 1964 when I was living in Wurtemburg, Germany, where I was taking an intensive German language course at the Goethe Institute. We had been having classes five and a half days a week. One Saturday afternoon a fellow student from China, Fritz, and a Nigerian student, David, and I decided to drive down to Munich to get away from the school for a few hours to have dinner, and maybe window shop and walk around a little.

We drove back about two o'clock in the morning. About half of the distance was on the Munich-Nurnberg autobahn, and the other half was on a *Landstrasse*, a country two-lane highway lined with trees on both sides.

We were driving along on the two-lane highway and a dense snowfall began. There was absolutely no wind, and the snowflakes were the size of baseballs, completely symmetrical – like lace doilies falling out of the sky! It was magical – I had never seen anything like that before. Usually snowflakes break up into smaller flakes, but these giant snowflakes just hit the windscreen – so that for a moment, we saw the perfect doilies land on the windscreen – and then they just faded away.

Now, throughout everything, no one said a word in the car, and there were no other cars on the road. It was January or February, and it was probably well below 20 degrees Fahrenheit. In other words, a blizzard was raging outside.

Maybe because of the monotony of driving, I got into a hypnotic-like, pensive frame of mind. David was asleep on the back seat and Fritz was sitting in the front helping me watch the road.

I began thinking odd, surrealistic thoughts: *Now, here I am in an age, when if we could really put our minds to it, this car could be completely computer-controlled and intelligent enough to drive its way back by itself, and I wouldn't have to get tired acting like a robot and wasting my time like this.*

Furthermore, I thought: *All right, what can I do with this time to benefit from it rather than just passing it and getting sleepy?*

Finally, I thought: *All right, what does the concept "the presence of infinite mind" mean to me right here and now?*

My next thoughts were about Bible stories that I had read a long time ago, for instance, about Moses and his talking relationship with God, as well as stories about Jesus. I thought about these things in a sort of stream-of-consciousness style.

Suddenly, over to my right about three feet away, I heard a voice that could have been baritone or tenor or alto – I don't remember which. It said very clearly in English, *"Slow down!"*

Now, I was driving maybe 30 or 35 miles per hour, and I couldn't see very far ahead – I was probably driving way too fast for conditions. I then looked over at Fritz, and he was still staring ahead. I realized he did not hear the voice!

To me the voice was totally aural, out loud. I slowed down to maybe 20 or 25 miles an hour. Within just seconds I heard that same voice saying in English, *"Drive on the left-hand side of the road!"*

I knew at that point that *whatever* was speaking to me must surely know something I didn't, and I had better obey it right then! So, I pulled over into the left-hand lane. Fritz looked over at me with a big questioning expression on his face. Within seconds, the road made a sudden, severe 45-degree turn to the right.

Being in the left lane, it was totally impossible for me to even consider making that right turn, because it was just barely out of the snow and it was way too late to do it. However, the headlights were shining directly ahead onto deep ruts that apparently farm vehicles used to access the main road. I was straight in line with them, so I went off the pavement and came bouncing to a stop some 30 or 40 feet from there.

David woke up with a start in the back seat. We all looked around, trying to gather ourselves together and fathom what just happened.

We discovered that about three yards over to the right of the car was an embankment of a river that went down about 10 feet at about a sharp 45-degree angle. Just around the bend from there was a bridge. There was no guardrail on that turn. It was now obvious to us all that had we been in that right-hand lane, we certainly would have gone straight in the river!

The mysterious voice, warning us not once, *but twice,* saved our lives!

David came over to me the next morning and said, "Well, I guess we both know what happened last night."

I said, "Yes, David, we do."

That's all the conversation we ever had about it. He and I shared similar belief systems.

There are a variety of possible aspects to explain this.

For example, I have always been of the mindset that you can turn consciousness to be receptive to truth, and, in this case, to a "presence" of sorts, which saved our lives. I think that you can handle problems and to try to live life this way.

Another way to look at it is this: I've become more acquainted with UFO material that we have been getting into at meetings I go to. I believe that we are sometimes intervened by an alien race that monitors us. I have read of these things happening.

In the end, I can accept more that it was as I first thought, namely, the activity of the presence of infinite mind in my consciousness directing me intelligently to do the right thing, which in this case saved my life. I tuned in with my ruminations on "infinite mind" while I was driving.

Also, people have suggested things like other entities that are disincarnate that work with us in life, like a guardian angel. I can accept that as a possibility as well, because I have run into that kind of thing in the past.

Commentary
Albert had an experience of direct voice, also called "audition" and "voice of authority." Direct voice experiences are most likely to happen in moments of crisis and at critical turning points in life. The voice, usually masculine, is loud and audible, as though it emanates from some point in space close to the percipient. It is commanding in tone and delivers a short, often urgent, message.

Direct voice experiences also come during states of meditation, heightened awareness, and dreams. The Bible has many examples of direct voice, as does the literature of saints, who spend a great amount of time in contemplation and prayer. Direct voices are also a significant feature of dreams that feature no visual images, only commanding voices issuing instructions. People also experience direct voice at moments of crisis, when a split-second decision must be made. Albert's dissociated, drifting state of mind while driving in the snow storm was an ideal condition for direct voice to happen at a critical, life-saving moment.

Is a direct voice a spirit, God, angel, alien, or one's own intuitive higher self? There is no definitive answer. It is up to the percipient to arrive at an explanation that satisfies. Ultimately direct voice experiences demonstrate our participation in a greater reality that transcends physical time and space.

CRISIS AT SEA
Dr. Tom Smith

A son and his mother share an intense psychic moment when death for one appears imminent.

I took a five-week trip around the world in 1970, and encountered a kind of derelict sailboat in Tahiti. I met the people on board the sailboat, and then continued my travels by myself through the Orient, Europe, and finally back to New York. Along the way, I got the idea that it would be fun to go on a long sailing adventure, even though I had never done more than a day's sailing and didn't know much about it.

I wrote to the boat people and inquired about going along with them from Tahiti to the South Pacific. By the time I got back to New York, I had a response waiting, telling me to come to Tahiti to join them. I naively packed my bags, quit my job, and, since I was working for an airline at the time, wrote myself a complimentary one-way ticket to Tahiti! Looking back on it now, I question whether I would ever go out on such a voyage again.

I joined the boat people in Tahiti, and we lived on the boat for about a month. The crew for the next leg came together, consisting of an American owner, the skipper; a German fellow off a square rigger, who had arrived on a square rigger from Africa, but didn't want to stay on it; and an Australian guy who had been sailing with his father, and decided he didn't want to do that anymore. Then there was myself, coming straight from three years in New York, living in Manhattan, and working for an airline.

Then along came a girl from California, a schoolteacher. She wanted to go, but nobody wanted her. It was kind of a guy thing, like when guys are sailing they sometimes don't want women on the crew. That was the attitude I picked up, but I talked them into letting her join in. Nobody ended up with her except the skipper, but we weren't really interested in that sort of thing. Four of us shared the watches, and she did the cooking until she got so seasick she couldn't do it anymore.

We spent about a month in Tahiti just playing around, working on the boat, provisioning, and taking side trips to the outer islands – to Moorea, for example.

The boat was called, strangely, *The Fearless*. Perhaps a more apt name for it might have been *The Death Ship* or *The Death Trap*. Here's why:

For starters, this was a 57-foot boat with an inoperative engine, a broken anchor, and a leaky hull due to worms. The boat took on water. We tried to patch it up. We had to use hand bilges (pumps), because we had no electricity on the boat. We had no lights except for kerosene lanterns. We had only a little speck of a light and a compass.

And, believe it or not, we had no lifelines on the boat. We never discussed any kind of procedures about "man overboard," if ever that should happen. We just didn't consider it. Imagine that!

Since the anchor was broken and there wasn't enough money to buy a proper one, we got a free one from the French Navy. It weighed 300 pounds. This was quite a bit of weight to haul up, especially when you have a broken winch.

When the boat had been refitted on the East Coast a year or so earlier, it was recommended that several feet be cut off each mast in order to make an around the world cruise. This wasn't done. That meant that when you had all the sails up, the boat became like a giant surfboard.

We left Tahiti and set out on the first long leg of our trip, a 10- to 14-day passage southwest in the direction of the Cook Islands, towards Rarotonga. Things were fine for the first few days. We were becalmed, which meant that we went nowhere, since we didn't have an engine. I was handling everything pretty well up to that point. Then the weather started getting stormy, and it just got worse and worse.

After several days of sailing in rough seas and taking turns at the watch, I was getting weary. I wasn't seasick, I wasn't throwing up, but I was definitely spaced out. Day after day, a strange feeling came over me. Maybe it was due to a fever and watching the weather patterns – and knowing too much about the condition of the boat – but I was becoming fearful of what could happen to us.

One particularly stormy night, I was asleep below and was suddenly awakened by a combination of an incredible thumping on the hull from water pounding against the sides, and yells calling me from above. As I woke up, I discovered that I had been lying out of my bunk right on the sidewall of the boat! It was pitch black and I was disoriented from being overly tired, sick, and worried about the weather.

I made my way up to the deck and discovered things had gotten worse and we were now in a severe storm. Later, it was estimated that we encountered something around a "force 6" wind, which is pretty fierce. Force 6 is characterized by long waves with white foam crests and airborne spray (by comparison, a hurricane is force 12).

All the sails were up, and we were racing along on our side, with the rail way under the water on one side. There were no regular wave patterns; it was really crazy. We were leaning way over and charging through the waves. The skipper was at the wheel, and the others were doing their best to get the sails down. We had no lights on board, so it was an unknown fury that we were dealing with, completely in the dark. We had no transmitter or any kind of equipment to call for help.

I was sent up front to the bowsprit, which was a five-foot wood extension on the front of the boat, to take down the foresail. Waves crashed over the bowsprit and put it completely under water. It took an incredible amount of strength for me to not only hang on, but to get the sail down.

It took me 20 to 40 minutes to get the bowsprit sail down with a tremendous expenditure of energy. With the help of the German guy, I was able to work my way back onto the foredeck. By then, I was totally depleted. I got to the mainmast, and I just slung my arms around it and froze, like I was paralyzed.

Thoughts started flashing through my head. When I had been out front there, up on the bowsprit hanging onto one of the wires, the halyards, I had flashed on where I had been just a month before: walking the streets in New York City, feeling really secure without any thoughts that soon I would be hanging on for dear life to the bowsprit of a sailboat at sea in the Pacific Ocean during a wild and severe ocean storm.

I realized that my entire life was in my fingers. If my fingers could not hold out any more and I gave up, I would be swept into the black night without any hope of rescue. The feeling of being close to death was terrifying.

At some point, something seemed to happen to my physiology, and my perception was that everything became somewhat electrified. I don't think there was any lightning going on. In a split second, all the other people on the deck became transparent to me – I saw all their organs and blood vessels, and everything. It was like having x-ray vision in the midst of my paralysis of fear.

It wasn't a hallucination, and I hadn't been taking any drugs. There was nothing else that altered my consciousness other than the near-dying experience and the environment.

Shortly thereafter, I regained enough strength to make my way over to the hatch and go below. After about 45 minutes to an hour, the rest of the crew managed to get all the sails down and everything closed up, and get down below to ride out the storm.

By the next day, the sea was much better, but still rough.

The x-ray experience was so strange that I could not communicate it to anyone else on board. They all had a bit more sailing experience than I, but they probably didn't have anything like that ever happen to them. I thought maybe they wouldn't believe it because it was so strange.

For the next few days, I had an intense longing to get my feet on land anywhere, even a deserted island, and stay put. I never wanted to go through this again.

A year to two after I returned home, I visited my parents. My mother and I talked about things that had happened while I was sailing at sea. I related the incident to her for the first time. She told me that at the same approximate date as my x-ray vision experience, she was hit by a flash that I was killed or in trouble. She had been lying down and the flash was so strong that she suddenly jumped up and was certain something had happened to me. Of course, she had no way to communicate with me.

I've heard of this sort of experience before, but I had never experienced it myself. I have no doubt that my mother and I had some sort of psychic communication.

Commentary

Tom and his mother experienced a type of telepathic connection that has been well documented in parapsychology studies. Telepathy is the mind-to-mind communication of thoughts, feelings, ideas, information, and mental images. It is closely tied to the emotional states of both the sender and receiver, and is likely to occur between people who have close emotional bonds, especially at times of intense emotions.

Researchers have collected numerous cases of telepathy for more than a century. The majority involve crisis situations, in which an individual becomes aware of danger to another, who usually is at some distance. Spontaneous telepathy occurs most often in accidents, life-threatening situations, and fatalities. The victim makes telepathic contact, often unconsciously, with a spouse, family member, or intimate friend. The information comes in different ways: as fragments of thoughts that "something is wrong;" in dreams, both realistic and unrealistic; in waking visions; in mental images; in clairaudience; and in words that pop into the mind. Typical cases include a dream or a vision of someone at the moment they die; a sudden impulse to go to someone's aid; the feeling that someone is depressed, ill, or dying.

In the case of Tom and his mother, his extreme fatigue, combined with an abject fear of imminent death, created a powerful burst of emotional energy that transmitted to his mother. At the time, she was probably in an early stage of sleep or at least a relaxed state, which facilitated her impression of danger. It manifested as an intense flash, or knowing, that her son was in dire danger.

The episode of Tom's x-ray vision is unusual, and perhaps can best be explained by his extreme state of body and mind, which gave him a psychic breakthrough.

EPIPHANY AT SALKANTAY
Mary K. Schreiber

A woman has repeating visions of a mountain
adventure that come true years later.

In 2006, for more than a year, I saw a vision. I would see it in my mind's eye like I was watching TV. The vision was me climbing a mountain with "three brown little holy men." I called them that, although I didn't know what they were. They seemed to have a spiritual nature about them. The vision of me climbing with these three little brown holy men on a snow-capped mountain played over and over in my mind.

I could be in the grocery store and I would see it in my mind's eye. I'd be having lunch, and again, I would see it in my mind's eye. It repeated so much that I said to a friend, "I think I might be going to South America to the Andes," even though I had no plans – nor would I have logically made plans.

At the time, I was living in California, and such a journey like that never originated from there. I kept looking for anything on the Internet, but found nothing.

Then we moved to Tennessee, because I'd gotten very sick while I was in California. In that process of healing, I did some energy work that helped shift what was happening to me. I was getting better.

I decided that I wanted to learn more about energy work, since it seemed to be so helpful to me. I knew that it was real. I did not necessarily really want to get involved in it; I just wanted to understand it better. I wanted teachers and a structured program, like a school. I went back online again searching for schools.

I discovered a website for a such a school. Unbelievably, part of the curriculum was to climb in the Andes! I couldn't believe my discovery! I said to myself, *Oh my God! There's my school!* It was a no-brainer for me.

I started that school and trained for six months to hike in the Andes. For example, we had to prepare our lungs, because we were going to go up to 17,000 feet. I was much heavier then. In the beginning of training, it was a lot for me to just walk a mile, let alone climb a mountain in the Andes!

My husband did the training with me. Since there is hardly any elevation in Tennessee we would hike as hard as we could. Eventually, we were ready.

I went to the dean of the school and asked for permission to go on an expedition, since hiking the Andes was primarily reserved for advanced students. Normally, they don't let beginning students go on these expeditions. Maybe it was my enthusiasm, maybe it was my persistence and drive, but I did get permission to go.

Here's what's interesting: there were three Peruvian shamans that accompanied us to the top to the base of the glaciers on the *"Apu,"* – the holy mountain – which is called "Salkantay."

Everything was just as I had seen it in my visions!

Hiking the Salkantay is the second most popular trek in Peru on the trail to the ancient city of Machu Picchu. The Salkantay is described as the wild feminine spirit. She holds that feminine essence or mystique in the holy mountains of Peru.

When we reached the 17,000-foot level, we found a beautiful glacier lagoon. It was like looking at the Caribbean – it was that beautiful and azure blue. We held our hiking poles up in the air in celebration, like we couldn't believe that we had done it. At night, the stars looked so close, you could reach up and grab them with your hands.

It was a transforming experience. I understood completely why I had had those visions. I work with corporations, and I had to deal with all this masculine energy, because I worked almost exclusively with all men. I would have to hold that energy.

Climbing the Salkantay put me in contact with the feminine essence of what was held in the mountain. I called in my female energy.

Climbing the mountain also shattered my fears about what I could do or could not do through business, and taught me that anything is possible in our physical bodies.

I never would have dreamed in a million years that I would really be doing that – climbing that mountain! But, I did have those visions, and they were fulfilled. It was an epiphany – my life changed forever.

Commentary

Mary's repeating visions of climbing the Andes, coming at a time when such an activity seemed implausible and impossible, have both a paranormal and a spiritual meaning. From a paranormal perspective, the repeating visions were precognitive, previewing an event that was going to come to pass. This is a pattern seen in other precognitions – the visions (or dreams) repeat until the event happens.

More important, however, is the spiritual meaning. Mary's life was out of balance to the point where she became quite ill. Her recovery led her to the way to realize the visions.

When life gets out of balance and individuals become deeply unhappy or stressed, the Higher Self provides guidance for restoring balance. If the messages are ignored, the imbalance eventually is corrected in a forceful way. In Mary's case, she suffered a forceful course correction caused by the illness and move – and then was presented the foretold opportunity to complete her healing. She had recovered physically, but she needed to heal spiritually.

This story is a fine example of the benefits of paying attention to intuition and psychic guidance.

THE IDYLLIC SPOT
Barth Wernet

A man spontaneously senses a curious, idyllic spot as he approaches
on his motorcycle, and gets a surprise.

I was on a cross-country motorcycle trip in 1983, traveling with my brother. We were both on BMW motorcycles rolling across Oregon, where we both lived, on our way back to Ohio, where we had grown up, and where my parents and many family members lived.

We wanted to make it an interesting trip, so we left Portland and took a diagonal up through Oregon. Then we went into Idaho, crossed the "Trail of Tears," (the forced migration of the Cherokee into Oklahoma during 1839-40), and headed up into Canada. We went across the Trans-Canada Highway, called the "Queen Elizabeth Way," a nice highway that at the time had one lane in each direction with a fully paved shoulder on each side.

When we came up on slower traffic, the drivers would see us in their mirrors and they would roll over on to the paved shoulder and let us go on by. We maintained a brisk pace, cruising at about 70 or 75 miles per hour much of the time. I did find out the top end limits of my motorcycle on the plains there in Saskatchewan.

Late one afternoon, we were just rolling along. We weren't in any place particularly notable – no town to speak of and we crossed a small river.

We came around a bend in the road, and there was this idyllic little stand of trees. Suddenly, an odd feeling of peace pervaded me, and I had a peculiar thought pop into my head: *You know, this would be a nice place to be buried!*

When we came around the other side of the curve, we saw a little graveyard there! We didn't stop. But I thought maybe I had experienced an interesting little "hello" from somebody's past.

I didn't get any sense of darkness or dread, but merely of peace and repose.

Commentary
This is a paranormal experience of an unexplained emotional rise and foreknowledge concerning an unknown location. Barth's natural psychic sensitivity tuned in to the energy of the burial ground and the tranquility of the location. Experiences like this usually happen when the percipient is in a distracted state and in good cheer. This seems to be an ideal state of consciousness for the breakthrough of something significant: a psychic impression, an inspiration, a solution to a problem, or a creative insight. In Barth's case, it was a psychic impression about the use of this spot for a final resting place.

PREMONITIONS AND OMENS

THE BUTTERFLY OMEN
Margo Bowman

A superstitious woman believes butterflies are a fatal omen.

In the summer of 1997, I was traveling in Russia and stayed in a small village called Klin. There were many villages like it – fewer than 30 people on the average, most of them over the age of 75. The residents had spent their entire lives there, except for those moved out by the Germans during World War II. They returned to their homes after the war.

In these remote areas, there were not a lot of conveniences. Many did not have electricity and had to get their water from a well or the river. It was a hard life.

During the summers, the people had to work on food production for the winter, like getting the mushrooms from the forest and putting them up. After winter set in, there would be no way to get supplies.

An old Russian woman fears the butterflies of death. Credit: John Weaver.

That summer, we visited an old woman, who spent most of her time sitting on her porch. When we arrived, she hurried us in and immediately shut the door. It was quite hot, and people usually left their doors open.

The woman looked terrified. "Shut the door! Go away! Go away!" she shouted.

At first, we thought her behavior had to do with the villagers' fear of being seen with an American or foreigner, because they didn't know what other Russians were going to say or do.

Then she kept repeating, "It was again, it was again."

We didn't know what she was talking about, but we got it out of her: the butterflies were circling.

We learned that she and her people believed butterflies were the souls of dead relatives. Symbolically, they had lived as caterpillars and become butterflies in death. When they showed up in certain ways, it meant your time was coming. This old woman had been under a butterfly assault all summer. They'd been in the trees; they'd been in the bushes; they got closer and closer to her home; and now they were trying to get into the house. She was convinced that when they finally got in, she would die.

It was late August, and we could see that this woman had not stocked any provisions for the winter. Even though she was trying desperately to keep the butterflies out, she seemed to think that they would succeed in getting inside before the onset of winter. Butterflies or not, without food she wasn't going to make it through the winter.

By the time we left the village, she was still alive and fighting off butterflies. I learned the following year that she died during the winter. Did the butterflies claim her – or did she starve to death due to her own folly in a self-fulfilling prophecy?

It gave me a new perspective on butterflies. When I see a butterfly now, I always wonder if what she said was the truth.

Commentary
The butterfly is widely regarded as a symbol of the soul, transformation, and rebirth. In certain circumstances, it can be a death omen. The most common death omens are black birds and night birds, and dogs that howl

in certain ways at night. Every culture has its own favored death omens, and for this area, the butterfly was it.

In folklore, the unusual or persistent appearances of death omens signal an impending death. The barrage of butterflies fits this predictive mold. The question is, would the woman have survived the winter if she had prepared her food stock? It appears that she felt no need to do so, for she was certain she was going to die soon. If she lingered into the winter and died of starvation, the death prophecy is still fulfilled. She might have died of other causes as well. There is no way to know if she could have escaped the fate predicted by the butterflies. In the end, do these questions matter? When it's our time to go – we will go.

VILLAGE OF THE DAMMED
Michael Brein

*A euphoric drive through spectacular scenery is suddenly tempered by an
overwhelming impression of grief and despair.*

The openness and freedom of a summer of travel may predispose
you to the possibility of having paranormal or psychic
experiences. They say children often experience these things, but
adults do, too. I believe that the Inner Psychic in me was particularly
attuned one day in the summer of 1963 as three of us, college friends,
drove through the magnificent and beautiful mountains of northern
Italy on our way to an area called Cortina d'Ampezzio.

Around every turn and bend was extraordinary scenery to
behold. Views of the villages below left us breathless, and we reveled
in the idea that this would never end, and that a continuous stream of
even more magnificent vistas lay ahead.

However, as we continued, I began to get an uneasy feeling.
I recognized from my life experience that I have had these sorts of

feelings from time to time, and that they do not portend anything good or pleasant. It's sad but true that the paranormal often involves unpleasant, negative, heavy, and emotionally-laden experiences.

The feeling built to a point that I was almost beside myself in fear of encountering something very bad. I just wanted to relish every waking moment of this beautiful journey through the mountains and wanted nothing negative to intrude into the pleasure of the trip.

However, such choices are not necessarily ours to make. Sure enough, as we negotiated a hairpin turn and came onto a straightaway into a mountain village, it all became clear. There ahead in our view was indeed the proof of my uneasy paranormal feelings that something terrible had happened here.

On both sides of the road, lining the hills, were empty shells – ruins – of nearly every building and structure we could see, attesting to a profound disaster.

We discovered that less than a year before, a monstrous landslide cascaded down Mont Toc, causing a wall of water 820 feet high to overflow the nearby Vajont Dam. The released floodwaters destroyed the village of Longarone and other nearby towns in the Piave Valley, and caused the deaths of more than 1,900 people. Sadly, the instability of the mountainside was well known, and a catastrophic landslide had been predicted at some point – but nothing was done. Ironically, the Vajont Dam was one of the tallest dams in the world. Only one-third of its contents spilled out, but it was enough to create a mega-tsunami of 50 million cubic meters of water. The dam itself remained intact.

The heavy, negative, emotional reaction to the loss of life that occurred there was indeed perceived in advance by my Inner Psychic self on that day. I wondered at the panic and terror that gripped those poor souls as they saw this watery wall of death rush down on them.

I do not relish experiencing the negativity of the human tragedies that occur in such natural disasters. Mine is not to question the why or the how such experiences take place, but to notice it all as if directed by some higher human good, value, or purpose. Whatever the reasons why I had this paranormal experience, my excitement of viewing the incredible Dolomite Italian Alps was certainly muted on that day.

Commentary

Michael had a psychic experience that is common in places where tragedies, especially unhappy or violent deaths, have occurred. The emotions of victims, as well as the psychic energy of the catastrophic events themselves, literally become embedded in the energy of the places, and hang like dark psychic curtains. Some visitors might be deeply affected by the residual phenomena, and experience a range of feelings from sadness to overwhelming terror and despair, to reliving the catastrophes as though they were victims themselves. Not everyone experiences the residues – a great deal depends upon the natural psychic and empathic ability of the individual.

Such reactions usually happen when visitors arrive at the location. Some responses can be explained naturally, for many people know the tragedy, and respond spontaneously with sadness and regret. However, in some cases, visitors know nothing about what took place at a location (for example, in places that are not historical sites). They find out later what happened and corroborate it to their emotional reaction.

Michael's experience has the element of premonition, which is a foreboding about a disaster that is about to happen, rather than one that has already happened. Perhaps he psychically picked up on residual energy from the past. Many disasters are preceded by premonition warnings, such as bad feelings and dreams. Or, the energy of sadness was still so heavy and pervasive (the disaster was only a year old) that he picked up on it well in advance of coming upon the scene. Perhaps his experience combined a bit of both.

BAD DAY IN BARCELONA
Michael Brein

A psychic hunch saves the day – a year later.

Was it my Inner Psychic that prompted me to get an alarm horn for my VW bus that day? Car alarms are practical, but when certain events unfolded months later, I had to wonder if my Inner Psychic had given me an early warning.

Fast forward nearly a year to Barcelona, Spain, where I was enjoying the sights. I had found it to be more convenient to park on a main street in a suburb of huge cities such as Barcelona and take the metro or train to the city center, rather than deal with the hassles of downtown parking. But there is the risk of potential trouble when you leave your car alone for hours at a time, especially when you have foreign license plates.

And so it was on that day, as on many others, that I did park-and-ride. I found a great spot right on the main street paralleling the beach and in full view of many people. Off I went, and plunged into a delightful day of touring the wonders of Barcelona.

At the end of the day, I took the train back out to the suburbs to retrieve my VW bus. Something was vastly different: I had a growing sense of ill ease. As I got closer to my stop, my feeling of anxiety became very strong. I knew something was dreadfully wrong, and I became quite worried.

You often know you are having a paranormal or psychic experience when a certain feeling of doom and gloom like no other makes itself known to you, and then all you can do is worry and become more anxious, if not even fearful. I knew these feelings, for I'd had them before. I was just about at the fearful stage by the time the train passed my bus parked on the street.

I glanced at it and sensed something was amiss, but I couldn't put my finger on it. With heart pounding, I disembarked the train and hurried to my bus. What I saw next created stark terror in me. Broken glass was strewn all over the ground. The little passenger-side window had been smashed. I opened a door, but no alarm went off! What happened to my alarm? I was starting to panic.

I turned the ignition but nothing happened – the engine was dead! I scanned inside the van and saw, to my relief, that nothing was missing. I started to clean up the glass and wondered what to do next. I had the feeling that whoever had broken into my van had departed in a hurry. Perhaps they were interrupted before they could find anything to steal.

An elderly Spanish couple approached me. "We heard your alarm on your car for about three hours while we were sitting on the beach," one of them told me. He explained that they heard the alarm go off while they were on their lunch break, and they came over to investigate. They saw two guys frantically run away from the van, jump into a car, and speed off. What happened, of course, was that when the burglars broke the window and opened the door, the siren began to wail and scared them off.

I was still amazed that *nothing* was missing! The alarm saved the day. But the window was broken, and the alarm had run down the battery. I arranged to have my van towed to a repair place. It was up and running the next day.

Installing an alarm system was the best thing I ever did. Thanks to my Inner Psychic, I was not the victim, but the "Superhero" – I paid attention to the forethought *a year earlier* to install such a terrific security system in the bus in the first place.

In an odd irony, before my visit to Barcelona, I once sat in my van on the border between Syria and Lebanon for about two hours awaiting permission to enter Lebanon. The border guard stuck his head in the engine compartment in my bus and admired the alarm horn system.

"Can I have this?" he asked. I didn't know whether he meant to buy it from me or that he thought he should have it for free.

I shook my head back and forth. "Oh, no... Not possible. I need this to protect my bus!"

It would have been easy for me to give it to him as *baksheesh*, a tip or bribe, to get on with my journey. But I think my Inner Psychic piped up again – it knew I would need it later, when my travels took me to Spain.

Whether you want to acknowledge it or not, the Inner Psychic is a powerful force!

Commentary
Michael's experience is an excellent example of how the Inner Psychic, or natural intuition, comes into play to ward off trouble, even months in advance. We are often prompted to take certain courses of action without having any rationale for doing so. Most of the time, people ignore such promptings – and then realize later, after the fact, that they should have paid attention. One could argue that installing a car alarm makes practical sense and requires no psychic urge, but Michael could have easily put the task off.

His psychic sense came into play again when the foreboding hit that something was wrong with his van.

The Inner Psychic is like a radar that constantly sweeps the time/space landscape, sensing situations that are forming for the probable future. It especially alerts us to potential problems. The more we pay attention to the promptings, the better we can avoid difficulties.

Everyone has this innate ability, in varying degrees of sensitivity. With attention and practice, it grows stronger and becomes more accurate. As Michael notes, it is indeed a powerful force.

PREDICTIONS AND FATE

THE GYPSY PALM READER
David Rivinus

An innocent psychic reading party turns deadly serious.

My father was an American diplomat in Turkey. People, including celebrities, businessmen, diplomats, and important persons, would come to visit Turkey, and it was part of my parents' job to entertain them.

One time, the guys went off and did their business thing together, and it was my mom's job to entertain the wives, which she just despised doing. She couldn't stand all the superficial conversations they had to have, but she did it.

They went to a restaurant, and a friend of my mom's brought along some of the wives of other diplomatic people who were also stationed in Turkey. They brought along a special guest. They chose a restaurant where they knew there was a Gypsy fortune teller. She was a palm reader, but she was much more than a palm reader; you could tell that she was psychically in tune and very competent.

The women sat and had a long lunch of incredibly delicious Turkish food. Then the Gypsy fortune teller came around and looked at everybody's palms and said some things that were translated immediately into English for those who didn't speak Turkish.

But when she got to the one special guest and looked at her palm, she put it right back down and went on to the next person without saying a word, and that was that.

On seeing this, the local diplomatic wives were a bit put out by this. It seemed very impolite. One said, "Wait a minute. You skipped this person, and we brought her along especially to have this reading. Can't you please say something?"

The Gypsy just looked at her and said, "There's nothing there!"

This added a sense of sobriety to the circumstances. Then everybody just sloughed it off and went home.

That woman died two days later!

I don't know why – it was probably some illness or a condition she didn't know that she had, possibly a congenital problem that may have been a heart thing or whatever, and nobody knew about it and it had never been diagnosed. Keep in mind this was 1953, and you didn't have the same kind of medical care that you have now. Some medical condition probably had been brewing.

There was no question in my mom's mind that the Gypsy woman read her palm correctly – and it wasn't the palm, per se. Rather, it involved the psychic contact between the subject and the psychic, and the Gypsy just read what she saw or felt, which was nothing! Then she moved on to the next person.

I'm sure there must have been talk among the other women about not doing readings with the woman again. They were probably skittish – after all, she might say something ominous about them!

Commentary
A palm reading involves examining the lines on a person's hand, which relate to different spheres of life, and to the past, present, and future. There is a Life Line that indicates whether someone will have a long or short life. As David notes, however, the Gypsy "saw" much more than was

on the palm. Good psychics "tune in" to their clients. A tool or method serves as a prompt or stimulus for a flow of impressions and information.

When the Gypsy looked at the palm of the special guest, she saw a blank because the woman's time was near end. There was no future.

Many psychics decline to predict the end of life, because it might create severe trauma for the client. We all know that someday we will die, but few of us want to know how or when. The information, especially if unpleasant, could be deeply disturbing. There is also the hazard that the prediction might not be accurate, for no psychic has a 100 percent track record.

The Gypsy's reaction was spontaneous. It wasn't an overt death prediction; she simply gave what she received, which was no impression at all.

Understandably, the others present would be reluctant to go back to the same woman for readings, out of fear that she might see nothing for them as well – and nothing would mean imminent death.

THE SIKH ASTROLOGER
Jesse Sartain

A mysterious astrologer with unusual eyes makes a stunning prediction
that comes true three years later.

I formerly worked as a photographer for *National Geographic* magazine, and they sent me to Nepal to photograph the Swayambhunath Stupa, the famed Buddhist Monkey Temple. I joined up with a Swedish lady, who was a photographer for a Swedish magazine, and we were going to do the photographing together for her article.

We were walking along the road from Kathmandu to Swayambhu to view the Stupa, just talking and photographing and experiencing. We ran into another person that I'd met previously. At the time, I had bought him a cup of tea and smoked some hashish with him, and talked for a little while about things in general. He didn't know anything at all about me.

He was a Sikh, with very long hair wrapped up inside a turban. He said he was an astrologer, and I had talked with him about that, too. He claimed he could read auras, (peoples' colors that they project), and also could read their foreheads, their hands, their feet, and, I guess, pretty much anything on their bodies that had something to tell him. But what was odd about him was that he had these strange blue rings around the outside of his eyeballs.

For me this was now an interesting second encounter, because he said to the Swedish lady, "Stick with this man and you will have something later in the future that will make you very happy! And I will write down the date that you will have this."

He then wrote down a date that was supposed to be important for this girl. She said, "Oh yeah, well, I'll keep it."

I said to him, "Thank you, but will you have a cup of tea with us? Will you join us?"

He said, "No, I'm very busy." And he left.

Years later, I was looking through my piles of mementos, postcards, and things that I'd never sent to my friends, and I happened to stumble upon that little card. I saw that he had written down the precise date of the first child I had with that lady, which was January 13! Furthermore, he said 5:34, which was the exact minute that my kid was born! I was right there photographing the birth, so I remember it very well. So, there it was, the exact day and time of my kid's birth!

That certainly freaked me out. How did he know?

Commentary
The Sikh had psychic ability, given his claim that he could see and read auras and get other impressions from people. He was also knowledgeable about astrology. Jesse said the Sikh knew nothing about him – and presumably nothing about his Swedish companion – but he probably picked up information and psychic clues and hits from talking to them and being in their presence. It is not common – but not unheard of – for psychics to make astoundingly accurate and detailed predictions, even years in advance. At the time, the two photographers had no inkling that they would have a child together. The prediction of the exact date and time of birth was highly unusual.

The blue rings around the eyes are most likely a natural phenomenon. Blue rings around the iris – the colored part of the eyes – are often a sign of cholesterol deposits in the eye. In a brown-eyed person, these rings would be quite striking, and perhaps seem otherworldly.

THE FORTUNE TELLER
Jeanne Long

A fortune teller's prediction comes eerily true.
Is it fate or self-fulfilling prophecy?

In 1989, right before I was ready to take off on a world trip, I went to a fortune teller in a bookstore in Florida. She told me, "You will have at least one encounter where you will meet a man with whom it should be a lot of fun and interesting."

I was thinking about just that at the start of my trip to the Far East, wondering if I really would meet a fun and interesting man. I began the trip in New Zealand, then went to Australia, Indonesia, Hong Kong, Thailand, and finally up into mainland China.

I met "Johnny" on the airplane from Hong Kong to Bangkok. I was sitting on the aisle and had my travel book open trying to figure out where I was going to stay in Bangkok. Suddenly, I had the oddest feeling that someone was staring right at me. You know, they say you

119

can tell when somebody's staring at you. I turned and looked, and sure enough this man, Johnny, was staring right at me!

And that's how this whole thing got started!

Johnny was younger than me – 15 years, to be exact. He wanted to know where I was from and where I had been, and so on. So, I told him.

Then he said, "We're soon going to land in Bangkok. Why don't you come with me, because I can get you through customs so much faster."

I said, "Well… I don't know…"

He responded, "I think you look like you've got to be taken care of."

I thought to myself, *Oh boy! Here it comes!*

Then I thought about what the fortune teller had said to me. Then I thought, *Hmm, maybe this is something I should do!*

We got through the line quickly and easily just as he said.

Next thing he said, "I got a taxi!"

I said, "I never take taxis. I always go on the bus."

He replied, "No, no, you're coming with me."

I said, "Well, I'll pay half."

He just ignored me.

We drove up to *the* famous and expensive Intercontinental Hotel in Bangkok – can you believe it? We walked in and I said to myself, *What am I doing? What am I'm doing?*

They didn't have the room ready, which annoyed Johnny, so he said, "We're going into the coffee lounge to have some coffee."

Regarding the room, I said, "I'll pay half."

Again, he just ignored me.

After we got into the room we sat there talking. I told him, "I've read this article in a magazine and about the Oriental Hotel. Elizabeth Taylor stayed there, and from what I've read, it's a beautiful, plush hotel. I'd really like to check that place out."

Johnny just picked up the phone and called the Oriental Hotel to make reservations for dinner that night!

I was starting to feel carried away – this was exactly what the fortune teller predicted! She knew what she was talking about!

I had an interesting experience the next night with one of Johnny's Thai friends, Perrot, who was a millionaire. We met him and went out on the town. The next night we were invited to Perrot's and his wife's home in Bangkok for dinner.

Johnny and I had a fling. I didn't know where it was all going, except that it fulfilled the prediction. I found later that Johnny was married to a Japanese woman, an artist who was older than him. Also, his wife had a lover – a man in Paris. It seemed they had an open marriage.

After I got back home, Johnny and I stayed in contact for a while. He came to California once on business, and he saw me. Another time, I went to Austria, and on the way, I stopped to see him. We went out to dinner. It was a nice time.

I told him, "John, you look older. You know, tired... Are you still married?"

He said, "Yes."

I said, "You're not happy, are you?

"No," he said.

I said, "Well, why then stay married?"

Commentary

The fortune teller's reading was accurate – that Jeanne would meet an interesting and fun man. Johnny certainly filled the bill. He was sophisticated, knew the local lay of the land, and was well-heeled. He probably was on the lookout for a companion for his Bangkok adventures, and Jeanne caught his eye.

It is possible that Jeanne self-fulfilled the prediction, which had put her on the alert for such a man. When she met Johnny, she may have encouraged the relationship, either unconsciously or intentionally, to see how it would play out.

There was nothing more to the prediction, no future, no long-term relationship, and that's exactly how it all unfolded. The sole purpose of meeting Johnny may have been for nothing more than a pleasant interlude. He aided her and provided entertainment. It must have been clear to Jeanne that there were no prospects of anything lasting, even before she discovered that he was married.

There may have been a deeper message for Jeanne, as well. Johnny was unhappy, in a marriage where neither party was interested enough to make a commitment, yet neither one wanted out, either. An open marriage may strike some as having your cake and eating it, too, but such a relationship can descend into a soulless limbo. Thus, Johnny provided a stark example of how not *to be happy.*

DEJA VU AND PAST LIVES

UNFINISHED BUSINESS IN TIKAL
Carol Griffin

A woman has unusual precognitive dreams that she feels fated
to act out word for word.

In October 1990, I went to Guatemala to see the ancient Mayan sites in Tikal. I had never been there before. The ruins of this ancient, pre-Columbian city are in a rainforest, and include some spectacular step pyramid temples. Powerful spiritual energies are present, a kind of earth magic. It's the kind of place where interesting things can happen – as they did to me.

A bit of background about me: I am a clairvoyant psychic, a gift I realized I had when I was about six or seven years old. I use my ability to help people get their own clear inner visions about who they are and where they are going in life. I'm a combination psychic and a metaphysical teacher.

At the time, I was living in Hawaii, where I had a lot of clients. I arranged with some of them that I would do recorded readings while I was at Tikal. Some of them sent me questions to ask on their behalf, and gave me small personal things to leave there for them. I was prepared to do psychic work for my clients, but I was not prepared for the personal psychic things that happened to me.

About 48 hours before I left Hawaii, I started experiencing insomnia, which for me, as a psychic, often means that a whole lot of electricity is going through my body. I was in a heightened state of awareness, and I was in a real – as I would describe it – psychic state.

When I finally did go to sleep, I had some vivid, lucid dreams with short scenarios. At first, I didn't think much about the dreams, except that they were very intense. Finally, I had a lucid dream about a young man. I thought I was watching a movie, saying to myself, *Who is that guy? I've never I met him.* I had no inkling that I was about to meet him in Tikal!

All of Guatemala is trippy. There are some 35 volcanoes, and seven of them are active. The day before we went to the jungle we were on Lago de Atitlan that was surrounded by seven of these volcanoes. I felt a magnetic energy that also helped to push me into an incredible space.

It was quite a jaunt to get to Tikal. It's in the Guatemala highlands, and you had to take a 40-seater small jet plane. You just got on, and then the pilot stuck his head in the back and announced, "We're taking off." The plane flew real low over the jungle and did not have air-conditioning. People were jabbering in different languages.

When we landed, I was shocked at the heat – it felt like a blast furnace. It was a different kind of environment that I'd never experienced.

On my first day, I met two men who were traveling together, a father and son. The son, to my delight, took a liking to me, and vice-versa. I had had absolutely no idea or intention whatsoever of meeting a man on this trip – it was the furthest thing from my mind. But from the minute I met him, I realized that he was the man in my dream! His name was Michael. He was an interesting guy, a firefighter from Washington State. This was his first adventure trip and mine as well.

Everything that I had dreamt about him began to happen. He started this conversation with me that was the same conversation I'd had with him in the dream. I was watching a drama unfold right in front of my eyes that I had witnessed in the dream! I felt like an actress in a play. I wasn't the writer – I didn't feel that I had made this happen – it just seemed *destined* to happen.

I'd had precognitive dreams before, but I had never had a dream where the dialogue with a real person was the same as in the dream! It was an amazing experience. I don't know if I liked it or not, because the ending was not what I would have wanted.

The whole time I was in Tikal I didn't sleep much; instead, I got into an exhausting hyper state, which put me in a heightened psychic state.

Getting into the park where the ruins were was quite a chore. We walked into the park every day, about two or three times a day. Just to get to the park entrance was a mile in the heat with the mosquitoes eating through your clothes. The sights and sounds and the smells were all intense and totally unfamiliar. Park rangers talked in Spanish and there was no food to be had in the jungle. It was disconcerting, to say the least.

When I found the right places among the pyramids, I recorded the readings for my clients and dispersed their items, which for one client was a lock of hair.

Meanwhile, I was midway into a two-day relationship with this fellow Michael when I realized, *Oh, everything in this dream is coming true, and that means that the ending is going to come true, too, which is not a very pleasant one!*

One night he and I sneaked into the park with a flashlight and climbed to the top of one of the pyramids, which was strictly against park orders. We waited, hoping for a jaguar to come. I had heard them around in the jungle, but I hadn't seen any. We looked up at the stars, and I had a sense of him maybe looking for a relationship with me.

Michael was a nice guy, but I was troubled because I had dreamed that I would have a confrontation with him toward the end of our trip. And that's exactly what happened. We spent more time together, and then he arranged to meet me to climb the pyramids together. But he didn't show up.

In the precognitive dream, we ran into each other on a pyramid and had a confrontation. That's what happened. Later I bumped into him on a pyramid, and I couldn't stop the confrontation from happening, even while I was saying to myself, *I'm NOT going to have this conversation with the guy that I dreamt about in the dream!* But that was exactly how the reality of it panned out.

In my dream, I had accused him, "You know, you really set me up to reject me. You made me think that you really liked me and you made plans with me. And you didn't show. Why did you do that? This was a two-day thing that could have been a lot sweeter, if you didn't play these games with me." I found myself saying those words, word for word, breath for breath.

That was it between us. I met him again at the airport, where I said goodbye. It took me a couple of days after I got home for that hyper state to wind down.

Sometimes you can alter dreams, but this one seemed fated to play itself out.

I believe that the trip to Tikal, along with my psychic life, were the catalysts for my precognitive dream. Tikal is a vortex, energy that the Mayan culture had infused into the place. Being among the pyramids can take you to some heavy spaces and heighten the experience of the whole thing. And, my being a psychic and a sensitive likely enabled me to pick up on it a couple hundred miles away and two days prior to my arrival.

Other things happened, too, things that I dreamt about during my two days there that came true within a few weeks of my return home after this trip. I won't go into detail about those because of their personal nature.

One of my clients wanted me to ask the Tikal spirits if the Mayans were taken away by extraterrestrial beings. She had always heard that the Mayans disappeared, and that there were no ready explanations. She wondered if it was possible that the ETs might have been mentors, and when they finished their duties, they took their Mayan students with them as their "graduation."

I got a "yes" response to that during the reading, along with more information about the Mayan interactions with a so-called higher intelligence and how they had come here to fulfill a certain plan which had to do with writing the calendar. They made a lot of predictions for what would be happening in our modern times.

The Mayans supposedly put all that down in writing as well as developed an extraordinary culture. While many walked away from it all, perhaps a lot of them were lifted off by the ETs.

I felt there was a vortex of a huge electromagnetic beam of some sort that had something to do with why Tikal was picked by extraterrestrials for developing a culture. There may be something to the ET connection, for Mayan culture has a tradition of worshiping the mothers and fathers from the heavens.

Overall, I did not get much feedback from my clients about their readings. I asked some of them, and they confirmed that the readings were accurate. I expected more; I guess the trip was more for me than for them.

Commentary

Precognitive dreams that preview upcoming personal events are common. The media give attention to disaster dreams that affect large numbers of people. However, most precognitive dreams are of a personal nature and pertain to events in a person's life.

The elements and accuracy of precognitive dreams vary considerably. Carol's dreams of scenes and dialogue that then played out exactly as dreamed, as well as word for word, are unusual in the literature of psychic dreaming. She states that she felt compelled to act out the dreams as though she had no control over her actions. It is likely that her experiences were intensified by the energy of the place that she felt, along with the spiritual energy of the ancient ruins.

Carol does not offer an interpretation of why this scenario played out with Michael, a stranger to her in a strange place. One possibility is that the meeting with Michael was a reunion from a past life, and involved a bit of unfinished business. Perhaps in a past life, Michael had "stood her up" in some way, and she never had the opportunity to confront him about it. The confrontation took place, enabling closure. The dreams prepared her for her "script," ensuring that no variation would take place. Closure had to occur. They parted company with no interest in pursuing a relationship.

From the standpoint of reincarnation, our lives are filled with reconnecting with many souls for many purposes. Some are major and life-long, while others are fleeting. People often preview meetings in their dreams. For Carol, reconnecting with Michael was significant enough to generate strong precognitive dreams. Perhaps whatever was unfinished between these two souls has now been put to rest.

DEJA VU IN SAMOA
Joe Mullins

*Were strong feelings of familiarity about an unknown land
a case of past-life recall, or something more ordinary?*

Haven't we all heard of someone, at one time or another, who seemed to know just what was around a corner in a place that they had never been to before? Déjà vu is spooky, and it never ceases to amaze me. But, as in nature and life, things are not always what they seem to be.

An early incident in my life that stands out involves a spooky déjà vu. I was in the Marines in World War II and was on my way overseas aboard the *Lurline*, a large ship. There were several thousand of us on board. Sometime around three in the morning, I was standing watch on deck as we passed near American Samoa.

A Japanese submarine spotted us, and we could see the trail of a torpedo heading toward the ship. We had a "general quarters" alarm,

131

and the ship took diversionary tactics. The torpedo went underneath the fantail and just missed us. That was heart-stopping enough, but it was only a prelude to a more profound experience that happened a little later.

It was a still, dark, moonlit night in the South Seas. I was looking off to the horizon, and suddenly saw a huge, black mass sitting in the water. It gave me the shivers. It was my first view of a South Seas island – the island of Tutuila, the main island of American Samoa, which is where the capital city of Pago Pago is located.

As the dawn light came up, the island shifted in color to gray and then into this incredible green that I'd never seen before in my entire life. I got a shivering feeling again and the hair all over my body stood up. Strangely enough, I thought, *My God, I've come home,* which was an odd thought to have out of the blue. I had no reason to think it. It was as if this was my ancestral place, rather than Ireland, which is where my ancestors are from.

A few weeks later, I was in the town of Apia, which is on the island of Upolu, which is part of what is now Western Samoa, an independent country. I was pulling a mortar cart while we were out on a military exercise, walking down a country road. Suddenly I had another strange feeling of déjà vu.

I said to the Marine next to me, "Hey, I know what's around the next corner." I couldn't get over it. I proceeded to describe a little house that would be just around the next corner, and when we got there, by God, there it was!

The house had a rather ramshackle tin roof and was a typical kind of dwelling you might find in those places. So, in a sense, it would have been an obvious guess – except that I gave specific, unique details about it. The Marine looked at me like, *wow,* and I'm not sure he trusted me after that. I must have weirded him out, and it kind of scared me, too. Why would I know this?

For years I wondered about this. Then I made a discovery that convinced me it wasn't truly a déjà vu experience.

When I was about 10 years old, I started reading books on the South Seas, and it's been a life-long preoccupation. Many years later, after the war, I was in a library, and I ran across a book that I had read when I was 11 or 12 years old. There was a photograph and description of this particular corner in Apia back in the 1930s. I must have "remembered" it when we passed by on that military exercise. So much for déjà vu.

The experience off Pago Pago on the troop ship was not genuine déjà vu, either, I think, but rather was what might be called an "ancestral memory." I have no Polynesian blood, however, so I don't see how ancestral memory could really be the case.

I am leery and even cynical about the whole concept of reincarnation, yet I don't exclude it totally.

What was it all about?

Commentary

Déjà vu – a French term meaning "already seen" – is a sense of familiarity concerning something that is unknown to the percipient. Déjà vu usually occurs during visits to places. A person goes to a place for the first time, and has the strong, sometimes overwhelming, feeling that they have been there before. They may even know the place intimately, without any rational explanation why. Physical sensations, such as chills, hair standing on end, electrical sensations, and so on, are common.

Déjà vu is often considered to be an indicator of a spontaneous past-life recall: the reason for the familiarity is that the percipient was there before, but in another lifetime.

Déjà vu has more ordinary explanations, too, as Joe believed. We can learn about a place and see photographs of it, which are "forgotten" until an event jogs the information out of storage. This is called "cryptomnesia," forgotten memories that seem new and original when they resurface.

Cryptomnesia is used as an argument against past-life recall, and it might be the explanation for Joe's experiences. However, there are other angles to consider that leave the reincarnation question open.

Joe's early intense interest with the South Seas has no logical explanation. In reincarnation literature, early and intense interests such as this are sometimes attributed to a past life, as are experiences of familiarity that have no explanation. Not having Polynesian blood makes no difference when it comes to past lives – they are not confined to bloodlines, races, ethnic groups, or generational lineages.

Three-quarters of the world's population believe in some form of reincarnation, but most Westerners do not. Spontaneous experiences such as apparent déjà vu open the door for some individuals. Perhaps there is much more to Joe's story that has yet to come to light.

REUNION WITH GRANDPA BRUJO
Angelica Chaparral

*A little girl meets a hitchhiking stranger who seems to be
her long-lost grandfather.*

This is a story about Vanessa, my daughter, who was about three years old, and this lover of mine, Shane, whom I had met in Big Sur, California, in one of the caves there. Shane was really a mystical, wild kind of a man.

We were in my Volkswagen van going to Taos, New Mexico. It was during a snowstorm, a blizzard, and Vanessa was asleep in the back. With the snow coming down, we must have looked like we were in a star ship traveling through the galaxy. We were singing Grateful Dead songs. We were stoned and high because we were very much in love.

Suddenly there was a Mexican man standing on the side of the road in his sombrero and with his poncho over his shoulder.

Shane pulled over and said, "There's a *brujo* standing there – a classic looking *brujo*, you know, a Mexican-Indian healer, a teacher, a sorcerer... A *brujo*."

I said, "Oh...Why are you pulling over?"

Shane said, "Why do you think?"

We opened the door and the guy got into the back seat of the van. He was Mexican-Indian and he couldn't speak a word of English. I thought he looked illuminated, like he was lit up by a glow or light around him – but maybe it was due to the snow.

Vanessa woke up, rubbed her eyes, looked up at him and shouted, "Grandpa! Grandpa, where have you been? Why did you leave me? I've missed you so much."

She jumped right across the car into his lap. Now Vanessa has always been very reserved. She only takes to a rare person, which is the opposite of me.

I said, "Whoa, what is this?"

A little background: My father died when I was pregnant with Vanessa, and my mother was already parted with her father, so Vanessa didn't know grandparents – any of them – since she was born. So why was she calling this stranger "Grandpa" like she knew him? Tears were coming down her face and she was so full of joy to see this man.

Now, here's what's strange: He was talking to her in Spanish and she was talking to him in English – they were *having* a conversation! Shane and I knew that what we were hearing was real, and they were having an entire conversation in two different languages! And they understood each other! He knew what she was saying and was answering her questions in Spanish, and she was answering his questions in English.

Shane, who knew Spanish, said to the guy, "Where do you wanna go?"

He said he wanted to go to a tavern, and told us how to get there. We pulled up to the tavern and he got out of the car. Tears were flowing down his face, because Vanessa was yelling, "Don't leave me again, don't leave me again, Grandpa! How can you go?" She was crying and carrying on. Then she jumped out of the car into his arms saying, "I'm staying with my Grandpa!"

I said, "Oh, no, no, no!"

She really wanted to stay with him. He gave her candy out of his pocket, and then told her in Spanish why she had to go with me, and how he and she would be together again later. Vanessa resisted, and insisted she would not go with me.

Shane and I got out of the car and parted them. Vanessa was so angry and upset. The man was crying and he left, and she was sobbing away.

She got into the car, and then I said I was so sorry. "What can I do?"

She said, "Momma, sing to me; don't talk to me, just sing to me." She was really upset and angry. "Just sing to me."

I said, "You want me to sing? Okay, I'll sing." I sang, and then she fell asleep. We continued on our trip and finally came to our destination. The sun had come up. Vanessa woke up and didn't remember a thing about any of what had happened with the man. She didn't remember the interaction, didn't say a thing, didn't want to hear anything about it, and didn't want to talk about it.

The whole thing was a mystery.

In thinking about it, it seemed to me that the man had to have been Vanessa's real grandfather, in some way. Vanessa's father was part Cherokee. I'm part Blackfoot, and the hitchhiker was Indian-Mexican, so there could be a chance that there was a roots connection of sorts. It's my theory that on this planet, whoever 'sews' must have roots together historically, and our seeds lead us to each other again. So there could be a real ground explanation for the connection that they had – even though it was a needle in a hay stack – one in a million!

Commentary
There are three possible explanations for what happened to Vanessa. One is that the hitchhiker had a sense of familiarity and comfort about him that seemed "grandfatherly" to the little girl. She may have had a subconscious need to connect with grandparent figures, who had been absent from her life. Shane called the man a "brujo," a witch or sorcerer, though we have no evidence that he was, or that he did anything to cast a spell upon Vanessa.

This explanation does not adequately address the immediate familiarity they seemed to share, as well as their fluency of communicating in two languages, if that exchange was genuine. Children at play, especially with invisible friends, will concoct "languages" that make perfect sense to them. Perhaps the old man, grateful for a ride in the snowstorm, was playing along with her, speaking in Spanish and pretending to have a real conversation that excited her and made her happy.

This explanation also does not adequately address the extreme reaction Vanessa had when it came time to part.

The second explanation is that somehow, across time and space, Vanessa and a real grandfather connected. Her mother, Angelica, does not comment on whether the man was familiar to her as a father-in-law. However, we would expect her to recognize a family member. This explanation is not likely, either.

The third explanation is that Vanessa and the man shared a past life: perhaps he had been her grandfather in some other lifetime. This is plausible. Children who have spontaneous recall of past lives usually begin talking about them between the ages three and eight. As children get older, spontaneous recall drops, probably because older children become more engaged in the outer world. We can speculate that through an amazing synchronicity – the one in a million chance, as Angelica said – a little girl aged three was reunited with a cherished family member from a past life. To her, the boundaries would be blurry as to what belonged to the present or to another life.

This explanation addresses the emotional intensity Vanessa experienced. In the literature of case studies of children who recall previous lives, they often get emotionally overcome when reunited with people and places from those lives. It also addresses the sudden ability to communicate in two languages. Knowledge of unlearned languages are documented in some spontaneous recall cases.

We'll never know the reason why such a meeting or possible reunion happened – why the forces of the cosmos brought them all together for a brief time. The meaning may be something for Vanessa to figure out later in life.

MAGIC AND CURSES

THE DEATH CURSE
Dr. David Irvine

A man dates an Apache woman and is cursed to death
by a disapproving relative.

I've had a lifetime of psychic experiences. Sometimes I've pushed the envelope in my own spiritual growth. One time, my emotions and desires got in the way, putting me on a path of potential danger and destruction.

I had a death curse put on me by an Apache medicine woman. It was around 1980, when I was working with the U.S. Public Health Service on an Apache Indian reservation in Arizona.

I was seeing a patient in the diabetes clinic for about a year, and her niece would bring her to the clinic, so I gradually got to know her niece. I was very attracted to her. I got to know her for a year, and then I asked her out. I knew it wasn't a good idea, given our racial and cultural differences – there was anti-white sentiment on the reservation. Also, I was a doctor and her aunt was a patient. Still, I really wanted to date her.

She agreed to go out. We drove into the white man's town near the reservation and had a drink. She didn't have any alcohol. On the way back she said, "You know, I am going get beat up!"

I said, "What do you mean?"

She said, "My aunt is going to be upset that I went out on this date with you."

I dropped her off near her little house, and the aunt came out of the house and met her at the fence. And as soon as she crossed through the fence, the aunt started hitting her and throwing rocks at her.

I was furious. Then a cop car cruised up – an Apache cop car – and I told the cop, "Look, this woman is beating up this girl. Do something about it!"

He said, "You'd better leave."

I thought I better do as he said, so I left. I didn't see that young woman for a couple of months. During that time, I visited friends in San Diego. I was in a freeway accident – I totaled the car on the freeway. I was lucky – I escaped with only minor scratches and bruises. Shortly after, though, I got very sick.

After I recovered, I went back in the clinic in Arizona on the reservation. One afternoon, I started to feel sick again. I went up to one of the nurses and said, "I've got to leave, I just feel lousy. I feel sick."

She looked up at me and said, "Your eyes are yellow!"

I looked at the mirror, and sure enough, I had yellow *sclera*, which meant I had hepatitis.

I was deathly ill for a few weeks, so much so, that people started to say that I looked like death warmed over. I lost a lot of weight.

About three months later, I was getting better, but still was sick. Then this young girl that I had dated showed up one day at the clinic.

I was surprised to see her. I said, "What happened? I haven't seen you since our date."

She said, "Well, my family took me away to another part of the reservation to get me away from you. Are you religious?"

I said, "Well, yeah, kind of." At the time, I was studying the Tarot in Western mysticism.

She asked, "Is it a powerful religion?"

"Well, yeah, it's kind of like Christianity; it's a powerful religion."

"Oh, good," she said.

"What's wrong?"

What she said next chilled me to the bone. "I think my family might put a death curse on you!"

Suddenly it dawned on me why I'd had the accident and why I'd been sick. "*Might*? I think that your family *already* put a death curse on me, didn't they?"

She looked uncomfortable and said, "Ah, well… yeah, they did, because they didn't want you dating me." She explained that it was her aunt, the woman I'd seen beating her, who hated white people.

She paused and said, to my amazement, "Do you want to go on another date?"

"The first one almost killed me, I think I'll pass!"

She persisted. "We could meet in the desert somewhere… we could be secretive, and no one would find out."

"No!"

She didn't push it, and left.

A death curse! I knew I had to do something. I had a patient who was a medicine man. I knew he was the real deal. Once, an Apache nurse had a teenage daughter who disappeared one night. Her uncle was the medicine man. He was in the hospital at the time, but he told her exactly where her daughter was – she was staying in the house of a friend on the reservation. He knew!

I arranged to meet him to see what he could do for me. I told him I had a death curse on me and explained the situation. He didn't speak English, so we had to communicate with the help of an interpreter.

"Come back tomorrow morning at 10 o'clock and bring 20 dollars," he told me.

I thought, *Now my patients are charging me! What do I have to pay 20 dollars for? Oh well, it's worth it.*

I came back with the money. The medicine man's little house had just a couple of chairs in it. We sat down. I asked, "So, do I have a death curse on me?"

The medicine man looked at me and said, "Yes you do – but I will take care of it."

I gave him the 20 dollars. He took the money, and that was that. I left. Whatever he did to undo the curse, he did on his own, by himself. I didn't know what to expect. I thought I might notice a marked change or shift, but I did not. I did continue to get better.

By this time, I had been on the reservation for about two-and-a-half years. A few months before I left there for good, the aunt who had put the death curse on me showed up at the diabetic clinic for treatment. On most days, there were five physicians working at the clinic, and patients did not know in advance which doctor would treat them. What were the odds it would be me?

When I walked into the room, she turned white as a sheet, as if she'd seen a ghost. She looked incredibly scared.

I walked over to her and she got up. I put my arm around her and said, "You put a death curse on me, didn't you? It didn't work, did it?"

End of story!

I found out later that there are "hexers" among the Apaches who put curses on people. The aunt and her family apparently thought I had put some sort of a love hex on her niece, which was ridiculous – we had one date. Their response was to put a death curse on me.

In retrospect, I see how my emotions and desire to get involved with the niece influenced me to override my intuition, and I got into deep trouble. To this day, I say pay attention, and be careful who your friends are!

Commentary

Cursing is a real and potent power. It is a magical spell done for revenge and to harm, causing bad luck, misfortune, illness, apparitions, poltergeist disturbances, disasters, destruction – and death. Every culture and society since ancient times has used curses to right wrongs, wreak vengeance, and eliminate rivals.

So important is cursing that many societies have professional cursers, as David discovered about the Apache. They are witches and sorcerers who possess abilities to use magical power.

A death curse causes a victim to die by illness or accident. It usually is an ultimate punishment for the most serious of crimes, however. Laying a death curse on a person for dating a family member is extreme – even if they were convinced a love hex was at work – and probably would not have been considered an acceptable course of action by others in the community.

Victims do not need to know they have been cursed for a curse to work. Sometimes the knowledge helps the success of the curse, for terrified victims contribute to their own demise. Using something personal of the victim – a photograph, piece of clothing, or snippet of hair – helps to establish a sympathetic magic link. These are not always necessary, for many curses can be thrown at a distance, much like praying for someone at a distance. This seems to have been the case with David.

The success of a curse depends on many factors. David suffered an accident and a serious illness, but fortunately for him the curse was not strong enough to kill him.

THE MACUMBA EXORCISM
Chad Deetken

Macumba! Or, be careful – you might get what you ask for!

In 1978, I was traveling throughout South America, every country except the Guyanas. I was with a woman, Sandy, whose family came from British Guyana, which is on the north coast of South America. She was mostly East Indian, but had been born in Guyana. She was also part Jewish and Spanish. She looked Brazilian, quite exotic.

In Recife, which is south of the mouth of the Amazon River, we were wandering around, and we had heard that this was an area where they still practiced Macumba, a Brazilian tradition of magic. We thought it would really be cool to experience something like that.

We asked around, and because Sandy was taken for Brazilian, people were friendly. We were in the outskirts of Recife, the poor slum areas, and people talked to us. Eventually somebody said, "Oh yeah, I'm going to one tonight – it's a Macumba ceremony and I'm sure you'd be welcome. Come back (at a certain time)." So, we did. And sure enough, that person was still there and said, "Look, let's go."

We went to a wooden house and went inside. It was devoid of furniture. We were taken into one big room with wooden benches around the outside walls. The central floor, which was wooden, was clear, and there were patterns drawn on the floor. There were candles stuck in different places. There were about 20 people, all Brazilians, sitting on the benches.

The room had two parts. At opposite ends, up against the walls, were altars. One altar contained positive spiritual images from different cultures: The Virgin Mary, Jesus, an Islamic saint, Buddha, Krishna, and so on. There were burning candles, and also photos. It was neat.

On the opposite end of the room was another altar, but it looked negative. It had demons, the devil, Satan, and people with pitchforks, etc. You could see that the room was bipolar.

Everyone sat down. No one made a big deal over us. We spoke to a few people, sat down, and the room went quiet.

The door opened, and an old woman, the priestess, came in. She obviously was a Brazilian of black African descent. She was not huge, but she was strong and had a strong face. She might have been about 50 or 60 years old – it was hard to tell. She was dressed in white with a skirt that flared way out, and she had a cloth on her head. You could tell she was very powerful, because she was paid a great deal of respect.

People started organizing. Most of the people were there just to watch, and some to participate. She had her helpers, and they did various things in the center, like taking care of the incense and the water. The priestess mumbled a lot of words we could not understand. She glanced towards us, but she didn't really focus on us.

The ceremony went on for about 10 minutes, and it was quite interesting, but, at that point, we didn't know exactly what she was doing.

Then everything stopped, and the door opened again – the door to the outside that the priestess originally came through. This time, three people came in. There was a man, who looked like he was in an altered state. Another man and a woman were at his sides, holding him up by the arms. He looked like he was having trouble standing. He was slouching and hanging on to them, and he was stumbling into the room.

I thought, *Wow! Jesus. What is this?*

They brought him into the center, and the priestess came back and worked around him and did things with the smoke, blowing smoke on him and saying incantations while the man and woman held him up. You could tell by his eyes, which looked weird and were rolling back, that he was either drugged or in an altered state. I didn't know which. But he was out of it – *really* out of it!

Then they went around and around him with the candles. When they stopped, we knew this was the apex of the ceremony, that something big was going to happen.

The priestess went up to him. The two attendants were holding him tight. She leaned over and went *whooh!* blowing into his ear, and at once stepping back. He completely freaked out and went wild. He was still in some weird stupor, but he wasn't in that slouching, slothful posture. He was suddenly energized, and he threw his arms out and tossed both attendants onto the floor. It was like he turned into a superman, completely out of control.

Sandy and I were sitting on the edge of our chairs, trying not to draw attention to ourselves. This looked serious, and we had no idea at all what it was all about. But it was cool, really wild! What a show of it! We were "cautiously scared."

The attendants got back up and jumped on the man, wrestled him to the ground, and held him there until he calmed down. Then the priestess came back and had the attendants move him aside.

Then this guy started wriggling and writhing on the floor. His hands and his feet became twisted, like the muscles had tightened up in spasms and curled inward, making him look very spooky. He started crawling on the floor towards the negative altar. He looked possessed.

The attendants grabbed him by the feet and pulled him back to the center. As soon as they let go, he started crawling toward the negative altar again. They turned him around to the positive one with Jesus and Mary.

However, he turned right back around and headed back for the demon altar. Finally, they just let him go, and he got real close to it. Just as he was just about to pull himself up on it, they grabbed him again and pulled him into the semi-circle.

They stood him up back up and then the priestess came back to him and blew in his other ear, and uttered more incantations. He instantly collapsed and was briefly unconscious.

The attendants helped him up. He then rubbed his eyes, and opened them, as though he had just come out of a deep sleep. He looked fine, but stunned. They helped him out of the room.

Then the priestess came over to talk to the audience. She came to us, and looked at Sandy, took her hands and examined them. It made us kind of uncomfortable.

The priestess spoke to Sandy in Portuguese, which Sandy understood. The priestess said she really liked Sandy and wanted to her to stay and become her apprentice.

Sandy wanted to get out of it diplomatically without insulting the priestess. Both of us smiled and Sandy said, "I'm really honored, but I can't. I have obligations. I have to travel – we're on the move." She repeated over and over, "I really can't." Finally – it seemed like forever – the lady just walked away.

We were both relieved once we got out of the house. It wasn't at all threatening, but the whole thing was very bizarre. And, we didn't want to mess with a powerful person like the priestess. We were very happy when it was all over and we walked out and down the street.

In hindsight, it was an amazing experience. We had never seen anything like this. The man must have been under a spell or the influence of drugs. I don't think it was drugs, because you don't snap out of a drug stupor that powerfully with somebody blowing in your ear. It had to have been a spell that caused him to be drawn to the dark side and possessed by a demon.

People like him came to this priestess and others like her because they had physical problems, they were sick, or they thought they had a devil in their minds, something with a pitchfork telling them to kill their wives or themselves, or something like that.

They sought relief in these rituals. They paid, I was sure, because it was a service. We didn't see this man pay, but he or his family probably paid before it began.

It was all very amazing.

Commentary

Macumba, which means "magic," is a Brazilian magico-spiritual tradition similar to Voodoo and Santería, involving the worship of African gods through possession of the spirit and magic. Prior to the twentieth century, Macumba was an umbrella term for both religious and magical practices, but today it refers mostly to magical practices, while the religious practices are known as Candomblé and Umbanda.

Macumba evolved when black slaves transported to Brazil by the Portuguese in the 1550s found that their tribal religion had much in common with the spiritual practices of Indian tribes along the Amazon River. The slaves were forced to adopt Catholic practices, but syncretized their gods with the local gods and Catholic saints.

Magical practices in Macumba involve spell-casting, such as to procure lovers, have children, gain money, harm enemies, heal illness, have good luck, get protection, and so on. There are rituals for exorcizing demons that take possession of people. The breath is used to effect spells and send spiritual power.

Chad and Sandy probably witnessed an exorcism. It is not possible to know what caused the state of the victim – his condition may have been the result of the possession. Nor do we know why and how he became possessed. His behavior was characteristic of possession cases.

The invitation to Sandy to become the priestess's apprentice is questionable, as it would be unlikely for a stranger – even one who looked Brazilian – to be solicited under such circumstances. The priestess made a show of reading her palms and presumably seeing something significant in them. There may have been more to it, such as an "apprenticeship" for a fee. Outsiders and tourists would be regarded as having money.

THE HAWAIIAN WAKE-UP CALL
Joanne Kaster

*A disrespectful tourist taunts the ancients at a sacred site
and receives a wake-up call.*

W e were visiting the island of Oahu, Hawaii in 1990. Some friends decided to go visit the Nuuanu Pali, otherwise known as the Pali Lookout, a visitor attraction area just off the main Pali Highway that connects downtown Honolulu to the Windward Oahu coastline. Madame Pele, the ancient Hawaiian fire goddess, is said to reside around the Kilauea Volcano on the Big Island of Hawaii, but rumors persist that she makes occasional appearances, in the guise of an old woman, walking along the highway area of the Pali on Oahu.

Legends assert that bad luck happens to those who flaunt Madame Pele's rules, the most important of which is to never remove rocks, stones, or sand from Hawaii. Post office personnel in Hawaii will tell you that every day, "stolen" items such as rock souvenirs are received from tourists around the world, who write that horrible things befell them because they offended Madame Pele.

Also, Hawaiian legend and history has it that hundreds of Hawaiian warriors were pushed off the cliff at the edge of the high Pali Lookout area, falling to their deaths hundreds of feet below. Their ghosts haunt the mountains.

I told these stories to one of my friends, who pooh-poohed them rather un-coolly, unabashedly, and un-surreptitiously.

One day we decided to go up to the Pali cliffs. I knew full well that this skeptical friend was going to disclaim and denigrate anything and everything supernatural. We took two friends along with us. When we got up there, he made fun and threw a quarter over the mountain, telling me that two dimes and a nickel came back to him! Rather than throwing coins as an honorable offering of sorts, his actions and tone were the epitome of disrespect.

We had locked the doors to the car, as it was well known that this isolated tourist spot was often the scene of car break-ins and pilfering. But when we came back, a door was wide open and all the locks were unlocked! Nothing was taken.

My friend got mad at everybody, accusing us of leaving the doors open and unlocked. We told him we had not done so.

He said, "You did, too!"

We all got in the car and left.

The next day we decided to go back to the top of the Pali cliffs again. I don't know why. Perhaps for the sake of my friend's ego, to prove a point, I guess.

We took the same friends with us. This time, my skeptical friend made it a point to go around the car assuring himself that it was totally locked up. He then said, as if to make a point with us, "Now, all the doors are locked! I know you haven't unlocked anything! You guys all go ahead of me."

Lo and behold, when we got back to the car, just as the day before, another door was open once again as if to greet and mock us, and all the locks were once again unlocked! Again, nothing was taken.

By this time, my friend was fuming. Both he and the rest of us had not a clue as to what was going on. We got in the car and he got even madder. He fumed that I changed his pre-set favorite radio station.

I said, "I haven't touched your radio!"

And that was our little ghost experience.

Commentary

Madame Pele is the temperamental and passionate goddess of the volcanoes, who easily becomes wrathful at thoughtless humans over their disrespect and theft of pieces of her "children," the volcanic mountains. Sightings of Pele, in the form of a beautiful young woman or an old, haggard woman, have been reported for centuries.

The returning of souvenir rocks to the Hawaii Volcanoes National Park has been documented since the 1950s. More than 2,000 pounds of rocks are repatriated every year. In the accompanying letters, the tourists usually say they did not believe in Pele's curse, but since taking the rocks home, they had been plagued with bad luck, financial loss, illness, and accidents. By returning the rocks, they hoped to placate the vengeful goddess and bring an end to their misfortune.

The tricks with the car locks, doors, and radio that Joanne and her friends experienced are typical of poltergeist phenomena that occur in haunted places. Perhaps Pele or her band of ghost warriors decided to yank the skeptic's chain.

THE DEVIL SNAKE
Dr. David Irvine

*A man ignores a warning not to touch a dead snake
and puts himself in jeopardy.*

Around 1983, I was traveling with a group in southern Mexico to study Mayan ruins and ancient culture. We were staying in a village of the Lacandon, an ancient tribe of pure Mayan. One day we were going through the jungle to see a small Mayan ruin when our Lacandon guide suddenly pulled his .22 rifle up and fired once at something about 30 to 40 feet away. We walked over and saw that he had killed a fer-de-lance, one of the most deadly, poisonous snakes in existence. They are incredibly aggressive, and will chase you.

Our guide told us that he had smelled it – caught a whiff of it – and that's how he knew it was there. He said that a fer-de-lance had bitten his daughter a year or two earlier in the village, and she almost died. He had an intense dislike of this kind of snake. It seemed to me that killing this snake was a personal vendetta.

Someone in our group mentioned that he wanted the snakeskin to tan or preserve and hang it on a wall. I thought, *Oh, somebody wants this hide? I'll help him.* I volunteered to cut the snake's head off.

The guide reacted strongly. "Oh, no, no, don't go near the snake, because it's a *devil snake*. Do not ever touch a devil snake!"

I didn't think anything of it, and I wasn't afraid, because the snake was dead. So, I was the first one to touch the snake after it had been shot. I stepped on its head and cut it off with my left hand because I am left-handed. I handed the gentleman in our group the snake's body. I don't think I touched it with my hand, but used the knife to handle it.

The guide said nothing, and I didn't worry about it anymore. As it turned out, there was much more to it than first met the eye!

About a year-and-a-half later, I attended a weekend workshop in Seattle on *Huna*, the ancient Hawaiian art and science of healing. It was taught by a Hawaiian *Huna*, an older woman in her eighties, who was famous, one of the five "living legends" in Hawaii. She had an assistant working with her.

We had to do an exercise where we listed everything that had influenced us in our lives – places, people, events – everything and anything we could bring to mind, so we could cut the *Aka* cords, the energy connections between something else and ourselves. By cutting the cords, we would cut the connections to our past that are a drain of energy on the present.

I was immersed in making a long list when the *Huna* assistant walked up behind me, looked down and said, "Don't forget to write down that snake that is wrapped around your left arm!"

I thought, *What?!*

For a moment, I had absolutely no idea what he was talking about. It took me a couple minutes to put it all together. Then it dawned on me! My mind went back to that event in Mexico. I remembered the jungle where I cut the head off that fer-de-lance snake with my left hand, just after the guide told me, "Don't touch that snake! It's a 'devil snake!'"

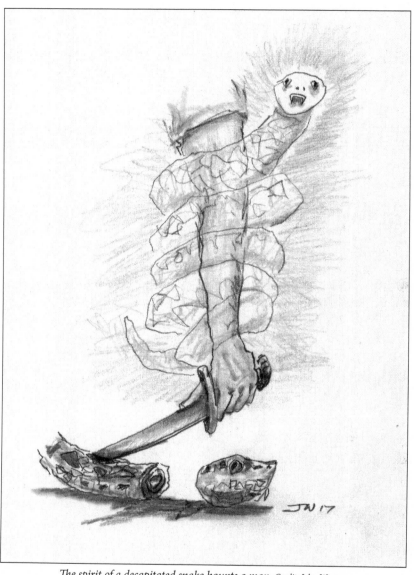

The spirit of a decapitated snake haunts a man. Credit: John Weaver.

Now it all made perfect sense to me. I now realized that the Lacandon guide knew exactly what he was talking about. Because I was the first person to touch the snake after it died, the snake's spirit attached itself to me, spiraling around my left arm. The *Huna* assistant, with his psychic third eye, could see the presence that was still there. I now understood fully what the Lacandon guide meant when he said the snake was a "devil snake."

I hadn't yet suffered any consequences of the spirit attachment – or so it seemed – and I proceeded with the ritual to cut its *Aka* cord. Perhaps I saved myself from something serious that was waiting to happen.

Commentary
Beheading the snake and handling its body caused a spirit attachment, a type of curse. Such attachments can be dormant for long periods of time and then come to life when circumstances provide the right energy. Hazards can include health issues, runs of bad luck, ruined relationships, and negative paranormal phenomena. The way the snake spirit was wrapped around David's arm suggests that health issues might have developed – or death by snakebite.

Westerners often dismiss the supernatural knowledge of other cultures as "superstitions," sometimes at their own peril.

WEIRD SYNCHRONICITIES

A TALE OF THREE FLOWERS
Albert Holdman

Three men separated by years and miles are reconnected in a bizarre synchronicity.

There are three Flowers in this story: a son, a father, and a grandfather. The first Flowers, the son, is my brother-in-law. His name is Elijah Beauregard Flowers, although we called him "Lesley." He was the youngest of three boys. The second Flowers is his father, Les Flowers. The third is Lesley's grandfather and Les' father. We'll call him the "Elder Flowers."

When Les was a little boy, he visited Kansas City, Missouri with his father, the Elder Flowers. The two of them were staying in a hotel in a room on the second floor when a fire broke out. With flames consuming the room, Elder Flowers grabbed his son and raced to the window. He yanked it open and called out to a man below. He dropped young Les down. The man caught the boy in his arms, saving his life.

163

Then Elder Flowers committed a tragic and fatal mistake all too common in the panic of fires: instead of escaping, he ran back to get his money pouch. He was overcome and died in the fire.

Young Lesley heard this story from his father, and the sacrifice of his grandfather made a tremendous impact on him. Without that sacrifice, neither he nor his father would be alive! He owed his very life to his grandfather.

When Lesley came of age, he joined the military and was sent to Panama. While there, he had to have a physical examination by a military doctor. The doctor interviewed him, and then got interested in his personal family story, and asked some questions.

Lesley related the story of the fire to the doctor, who looked at him in total astonishment and said, "Lesley, I am the man who caught your father!"

Commentary
This is one of the most unusual types of synchronicity, a meaningful coincidence with astronomical odds of happening. The purpose of these events is often hard to fathom. They can lead to new and significant relationships that were, perhaps, fated to happen. Or, they occur simply to demonstrate how intricately interconnected we all are.

THE IRISH GIFT
Art Hanlon

A man reconnects to persons from his past through a rare combination of synchronicity and clairvoyance.

My story has a bit of sadness because the people in it are gone from this earth. For some strange reason, I was involved in their passing.

The story goes back to the mid-1960s, when I was a struggling musician living on a shoestring in New York City. All I could afford was a two-bedroom apartment in a condemned building. The rent was about a dollar a month. The whole building was filled with writers, artists, actors, and freelance philosophers – people who later would be known as "street people."

Despite of our poverty, we had a fine time. It was a period of social experimentation. I was a folk singer, playing guitar and writing songs as well as doing other things. We would typically work all night writing or doing something else, and then we would sleep during the day.

165

Our building was located on 46th Street in an area called "Hell's Kitchen," a neighborhood on the west side of Midtown Manhattan that stretched from about 34th Street roughly up to 72nd Street, west of Eighth Avenue. The movie *West Side Story* was filmed there.

Hell's Kitchen formed in the nineteenth century when it became an Irish slum filled with immigrants who had escaped the great potato famine in Ireland. The place was lawless back then. In the 1960s, it was still predominantly Irish, and still a tough neighborhood – but nothing like it used to be. I think I resonated with the area because I have Irish blood myself.

On the first floor, there were a couple of apartments rented by actors, and one apartment by a couple who spent much of their time strung out on methamphetamine, or speed. They were Ronnie Annarunma and his girlfriend, who was from Germany. I did not have much interaction with them – I talked to Ronnie a few times in the hallway. I recall once seeing them getting into their car. I remember one day when Ronnie's brother came to visit. He wanted to get Ronnie back on the straight and narrow, but I don't think he had much effect.

Fast forward five years to 1968. I had left New York City and was driving across the country in my pickup truck. One day in Arizona, I was cruising on a two-lane highway in a desolate, middle-of-nowhere between Flagstaff and Winslow. I started to climb up a long grade. If you've driven in Arizona, you know what that's like. You can see the crest of a hill off in the distance, and you are slowly gaining altitude as you approach it, but it takes a while because it's far away.

I was driving along, and I suddenly noticed a flashing light in my rearview mirror. It was not a cop car, but a red light blinking on top of a little station wagon, traveling at a high speed. The wagon caught up to me and as it passed I saw a sign on the door that said "County Coroner."

I said to myself, *Oh damn, wow! He's sure going somewhere fast! Hope he's coming back!* But the flashing red light did not go *over* the top of the hill – it just *stayed* on the hill, and I started to get closer to it.

When I got to the top of the hill, I was horrified to see this incredible wreckage on the highway – a twisted jumble of two cars that apparently had a head-on collision. They must have been going very fast, because it was an unbelievably twisted wreck.

I don't know why, but suddenly the images of Ronnie Annarunma and his girlfriend popped into my mind.

I had not interacted with them much back in New York, and that was five years earlier. I hadn't even thought about them at all since then, but now the names of Ronnie and his girlfriend popped into my mind along with their images.

I slowed down to look at the wreckage. I don't know what made me do it, because usually I would just drive past things like this. I saw on the ground two bodies covered up by sleeping bags, and a state trooper standing there looking very somber.

I don't know what made me stop, but I did, because the memory of Ronnie Annarunma was so insistent that I couldn't resist it. I had to stop. It was like pulling me over there!

I went over to the trooper. I didn't want to come across as an "accident ghoul," so I was very polite, and I said to him, "I know this is very strange, but I think I know these people!"

All that was visible were two sleeping bags and two feet sticking out from under the sleeping bags. One was male and one was female.

I knew what the trooper would probably think, so I said, "I don't want to see the bodies. I don't want to ask any questions. But if I tell you a name will you confirm or deny?"

He shrugged and said, "Sure."

"Ronnie Annarunma."

His jaw dropped. He looked at the notes he was taking. He had Ronnie's wallet in his hand. He said, "That's who it is!"

I couldn't do anything more. I had a few more words with the coroner and the state trooper. They were dumbfounded, scratching their heads saying, "How the hell did he know this?"

I got in my truck and I had a very, very thoughtful drive on the rest of the trip to California. How could I explain this to myself?

I thought that somehow, in my state of mind at the time, I had guessed, and by some weird coincidence I had guessed right. I had seen one of the license plates, and it was from New York State. But that alone would not necessarily have made me think of Ronnie – I had only seen his car one time, and years had elapsed.

The only thing that made sense to me was something that was supposed to be part of my Irish heritage – the *Irish gift*, or second sight, the psychic ability to perceive things beyond the senses. I believe I have it, but I have let my rational mind suppress it. I have had incidents in my life where I knew things that I was not capable of knowing. The experiences mostly involve my children. For example, when they were young, I was able to "see" the kinds of lives they were going to have. I also have had psychic experiences involving myself, but that's a story for another day.

Commentary

What are the odds that you would be driving on a remote highway and come upon a fatal accident – and automatically know who the victims were? Furthermore, what are the odds that the victims would be people from your past a couple of thousand miles away, individuals you had barely known and hadn't seen for five years? Fate works in strange ways.

Art is right – his innate psychic ability was triggered by this event. We will never know how or why. Usually, psychic links form as part of emotional bonds, which is why two individuals who are close to each other emotionally, also by blood, can sense the other's thoughts and know when one or the other is in danger. These kinds of experiences have been studied for more than a century in psychical research.

From Art's description, he had no emotional ties to Ronnie and his girlfriend. He did, however, have a strong emotional tie to that period in his past, which he describes with great energy and fondness. That may have provided the odd, synchronistic link that enabled him to make the connection.

There may have been something else at work in this experience. Art admitted that he had squelched his psychic gift, which is not uncommon. Western society, ruled by rationalism, denies the psychic faculty. Perhaps the universe, or mysterious powers that be, arranged for Art to have this synchronicity experience as a way of reawakening and coming to terms with a gift he should be using in his life.

THE ASHLAND CONNECTION
Michael Brein

A man experiences an unusual five-part synchronicity
with astronomical odds.

Part 1: The Odds

Nearly everyone I have ever met has had at least one odd synchronicity experience in his or her travels or everyday life. By this I mean that an apparently meaningful coincidence beyond the normal probabilities of chance happens to all of us at one time or another.

They say there are more stars in our vast universe than there are grains of sand on all the beaches and deserts of Planet Earth. Of course, it is hard to believe (and impossible to prove). And they also say that there are no accidental coincidences – they all must mean something in our lives, even if they seem insignificant – and that the likelihood of such unbelievable coincidences happening strictly by chance is infinitesimal, say, one in a million or so!

Now, that may hold true for a single coincidence. Let's suppose that you have a complex synchronicity event that is compounded with two intertwined coincidences. The likelihood of such a compound synchronicity occurring by chance decreases the odds significantly, say, to one in a billion.

Now, let's say that you have a combined synchronicity experience involving more than three intertwined events. What are the odds of that happening? One in a trillion?

Now, consider what happened to me – a quintuple complex coincidence! My travel synchronicity story involves five unbelievable levels of meaningful coincidences, all intertwined and all happening at once! How is that possible? And what are the odds of that happening to anyone?

Now, I posit to you that the chance of what happened to me in this story is so unbelievable and unlikely, that the odds may be more than one in as many grains of sand on all the beaches and deserts on the earth – and therefore, possibly more than all the galaxies, stars, and planets that populate our universe! I say to you that such an experience that happened to me is not only possible – it really did happen!

Hard to believe? Read on and decide for yourself.

Flight to Philadelphia – *Hemispheres*, May Issue

I was traveling at the end of May from Ashland, Oregon to New York City to attend the BookExpo America annual publishing trade show, where I was to display and promote my travel guide series, *Michael Brein's Travel Guides to Sightseeing by Public Transportation*. My itinerary was to fly on United Airlines from Medford, Oregon, first to Philadelphia (to visit my sister for a few days), then take the train from Philly to New York, attend the book show, and then fly back from New York to Medford on United. I would be returning at the beginning of June.

On my first United Airlines flight from Medford, I picked up the May issue of United's inflight magazine, *Hemispheres*, to look at later. I intended to write to the magazine editors to inform them about my travel guide series and ask if they would publish a brief mention or a review.

Train to New York – The "Rahway" Sign
On the train from Philly to New York, I passed a town called Rahway, New Jersey. I remember glancing at the sign and recalling that I knew someone from Rahway some 42 years earlier, when I attended Carnegie Mellon University (formerly Carnegie Tech).

Then I attended BookExpo America in New York City.

Flight to Medford – *Hemispheres*, June Issue
On the return flight west, I grabbed a copy of the new June issue of *Hemispheres* and put it in my attaché case, again intending to read it later and then write to the editors. It was a long shot, and certainly very much wishful thinking on my part. No harm in trying, right? What were the chances they would do that?

Part 2: The "Coincidences"

Coincidence #1
I arrived home in Ashland. The first thing I did was go to my kitchen counter to look over the pile of waiting mail. I spotted a large white envelope with the return address from *Hemispheres*. Hmm, that was strange. *What could this be*, I wondered? I opened the envelope, and to my total surprise, it was a copy of that very June issue that I had just grabbed on the flight back, but had not yet read.

Interesting coincidence, I mused. That selfsame magazine I had right in my briefcase!

Coincidence #2
It does not stop there, however. I *never* had a copy of that magazine mailed to me – especially when I just happened to have saved that very same issue on my return flight.

Attached to it was a business card with the words, "Courtesy of the Editor. See page (such and such)." I eagerly opened the magazine, and to my total astonishment, there it was – *a review of my travel guide series!* Wow! And I hadn't even opened the magazine on the flight! Nor had I yet written to them to suggest a review. I was shocked.

Coincidence #3

I went upstairs to my loft office to check my email on my computer. As expected, there were some online orders for my travel guides awaiting my attention while I was away. They could be from Anywhere, USA... Europe, Egypt, Hong Kong, Australia. Lo and behold – an order from *Ashland* – right where I lived – my very own hometown – was waiting for me! I had *never* had an online order from where I lived. Simply unbelievable!

Coincidence #4

I looked at the order and got another shock. The name of the person was the same last name as the person I knew in Pittsburgh some 42 years earlier at Carnegie Mellon – and the same person from Rahway, whom I thought of when my train passed the sign on the way to New York. Was this order really from that very same person? And now living in *my* own town? And ordering my guides online? I laughed, because the notion was simply absurd to me.

But the coincidences still did not end there. I emailed back and offered to personally deliver their order. Remember, this order could have been from *anywhere* in the world. I joked and asked if I should deliver it personally to them – door-to-door service!

Or, would they prefer to pick it up at my place – an interesting llama ranch on top of one of the local mountains? For you see, I don't think that they had any idea that they were ordering my travel guides online from literally just around the corner from them!

They elected to pick it up at my house!

I asked in the next email, could the man possibly be that same person I knew once upon a time, some 42 years earlier at Carnegie Mellon?

I received an almost immediate telephone call back. I heard a voice say energetically and enthusiastically, "I would indeed be that person!"

To my incredible amazement, I recognized the voice! It was indeed Jan C. Now, honestly, I never had but a few conversations with Jan C. back in those days at Carnegie Mellon. Yet I recognized his voice after 42 years.

I was so taken aback by this that I sang to him the fraternity song. Now, what was amazing about that feat was that I could never remember the words to songs, let alone the words to one so obscure from an era 42 years back – but the words flowed, nonetheless.

Jan C. and his wife came over and picked up their guides. We had a brief reunion from some four decades earlier, marveling at this set of sheer unbelievable coincidences!

Coincidence #5

I asked them how they happened to hear about my travel guides and why they were interested in them. They said that they were into public transit, so when they read about my series in *Hemispheres* while on a recent United flight, they were prompted to order a couple of copies. Jan C. had not recognized my name, nor did he know that I lived in the same small town. And, he and his wife most certainly had no inkling at all of the incredible coincidences that made up my compound synchronicity – the "Ashland Connection."

The impossibility of this quintuple synchronicity was not at all lost on them, either. After all, they were statisticians!

Commentary
Michael's experiences form an unusual web of synchronicity – circumstances either unrelated or tenuously related to one another that come together in a powerful and meaningful way.

Synchronicity is the unifying principle behind "meaningful coincidences." The concept is integral to Eastern thought, but in Western thought it runs contrary to traditional "laws" of cause and effect. The concept of synchronicity was developed largely by Carl G. Jung, who termed synchronicity "an acausal connecting principle" that links seemingly unrelated and unconnected events. Jung credited his inspiration to Albert Einstein, whom he met on several occasions in the early twentieth century. Later, in the mid-1920s, Jung was probing the phenomena of the collective unconscious and encountered numerous synchronicities he could not explain. They were, he said, "'coincidences' which were connected so meaningfully that their 'chance' concurrence would represent a degree of improbability that would have to be expressed by an astronomical figure."

Jung said synchronicity occurs in events that are meaningfully but not causally related (that is, they do not coincide in time and space), as well as in events that do coincide in time and space and have meaningful psychological connections. In addition, synchronicity links the material world to the psychic realm. Synchronistic events, Jung said, "rest on an archetypal foundation."

F. David Peat, a holistic physicist and author, has observed that synchronicity appears naturally to a mind that is constantly sensitive to change. Travel opens a person to change and heightens sensitivity. A person who is also more psychically attuned, such as Michael with his Inner Psychic, would be even more likely to experience unusual synchronicities.

The question people often ask in the wake of a synchronistic event is, "What does it all mean?" Sometimes the connections are obvious and relate to issues going on in a person's life, such as synchronicities that solve problems. In most cases, however, the purpose of a synchronicity is more elusive, other than the "wow" factor.

Perhaps the true meaning behind synchronicities is an awareness of the profound interconnections of everything in life and the cosmos. We live in a constant flow of unfoldment that stretches out to infinity, and all things rest in an ever-present now. Synchronicity shapes a more holistic view of the flow of life, even a more Zen-like view, which appreciates the moment just for the moment itself, and nothing more.

The more we are aware of synchronicities in our lives, whether they be small or grand and complex, the more synchronicity is likely to happen. Message from the universe: stay tuned.

MYSTERIES AND TIME SLIPS

LOST IN SPACE AND TIME
Ken Stilgebouer

A man sets out on the road, experiences missing time, and winds up in the wrong state at the wrong event.

Every year I attend the Mothman Festival in Point Pleasant, West Virginia, which occurs on the third weekend in September. The festival celebrates a wave of strange activity that occurred in the area in 1966-67, featuring a winged humanoid dubbed "Mothman," lots of UFO activity, and all sorts of paranormal phenomena. Point Pleasant and the area around it are quite haunted. The town is small, and has one hotel, the Lowe, which is haunted.

In 2015, a man I will call "Ron" showed up at the Lowe on the eve of the festival, quite confused about where he was. Here is his story as he related it to me, and as I and friends of mine witnessed:

Ron woke up in his home in Indiana, excited about getting on the road. It was Friday, September 18, and he was going to the

2015 Sentinel Summit in Greenville, South Carolina. Ron had joined Heritage Action for America so that he could support the Republican goals of limited government and a better America. Ron was excited to know that he would be able to see the Republican Presidential candidates speak on Friday night and then attend regional breakout groups for the Sentinels on Saturday so that they could further plan their activities for the upcoming election.

Ron's bags were packed, his leather portfolio was filled with all his important Sentinel documents, he had his GPS, and he was ready to drive to Greenville. The drive seemed simple enough. Take I-65 to I-64 to I-75 to I-40 to get dumped into Greenville. It would be a long drive – 10 hours – to cover 670 miles, but if he left at 6 AM he should arrive in time for the Presidential candidate speeches that began at 5 PM. As it was, Ron didn't get out the door until after 8 AM, and was now hoping he would be able to attend a few of the later speeches.

It was 2 PM when Ron rolled into Louisville. He stopped for a quick bite, got back in the car and continued on I-65 as it veered to the east and turned into I-64. Ron was now heading for Lexington where he had planned to merge onto I-75 and continue south towards Greenville. Ron noticed that he was beginning to lose some time and that he should hurry if he was going to attend any of the speeches. He failed to notice that there was something wrong with the GPS and that it was no longer directing him to his destination.

Speeding past the I-75 turnoff, he continued east on I-64. It was close to 5 PM when he hit Huntington, West Virginia, and he was now worried that he might not be going the correct way to Greenville. The GPS had failed completely and now only showed a green background with no streets. Ron figured that if he continued to follow I-64 east it would eventually take him to I-95 where he could turn south again and head for Greenville.

It would be nice to have a map, Ron thought and he exited from the highway in Huntington to search for one. Finding a map would prove to be a challenge. Ron checked drug stores, liquor stores, grocery stores, and gas stations without luck. He finally found a West Virginia map and, satisfied with that, decided to move on. At least he would get to Virginia.

By the time his map search was over, the sun had set and Ron was driving east on Route 2 parallel to I-64. He figured he'd catch

Route 60 back to I-64 and would be back on track. Fatigue had set in, however, and Ron then missed his turn and continued on Route 2 as it slowly turned north to Point Pleasant. With the fatigue came the confusion. *I should have planned this better,* Ron muttered to himself.

It was late when Ron arrived in Point Pleasant. He spied the Lowe Hotel and decided to book a room. It was the annual Mothman Festival weekend, and normally all rooms are booked months in advance. Fortunately for Ron, a single room was available due to a late cancellation.

While he was checking in with Marcia Finley, the daughter of hotel owners Rush and Ruth Finley, Ro (Rosemary Ellen Guiley) and her husband, Joe (Redmiles) arrived, much later than usual, and came up to the desk. Ro speaks at the festival every year, and Joe is master of ceremonies.

Ron was talking about being in town for "the meeting." Marcia assumed he was with the Mothman Festival and pointed to Ro and said, "Here's one of your fellow speakers."

Turning around, Ron said to Ro, "Ah, then you must be a Sentinel." Ro looked at Ron quizzically and responded that she was a speaker at the Mothman Festival and that maybe he was here for another conference. Confused, Ron thought that maybe he might be in the wrong town and asked how far he was from Interstate 95. Ro responded, "A long way," and Ron was more mixed up than ever.

Ron took his bags to his room and wandered out to find something to eat. He was not sure if he was in Greenville, South Carolina or Point Pleasant, West Virginia.

Later in the evening, Ro and Joe were having a late dinner at the Iron Gate when they met up with me and a mutual friend, Lee, and we joined them for a glass of wine. Ro mentioned that there must be another conference in Point Pleasant because she had met a man who thought she was a "Sentinel" at some kind of event. We all thought it was peculiar.

The Mothman 5K was run from outside of the Lowe hotel on Saturday morning at 8 AM. Lee and I ran the course. There was some time after the run and prior to the award ceremonies for a quick breakfast, so we dashed inside the hotel to fill up on sausage, biscuits, bacon, gravy, eggs, hash browns, and coffee.

In the buffet line, a tall, well-dressed and trim man began to chat with us. It was Ron. We were heading to a table to sit and eat when Ron asked if maybe "the meeting" was behind the swinging doors where other diners were eating. I said, "I doubt it," and so Ron joined us for breakfast.

Ron then told us his story of getting lost, his GPS failing, and taking forever to find a map. Once he did find a map he was finally able to get to where he needed to be – or so he was convinced. It was so confusing, all the driving around, but he was here now and able to attend "the meeting."

During the discussion, Ron never made eye contact. I looked at Ron's eyes and could see the confusion as if he thought he was in the right place but knew something was very wrong about it. Ron told us that it took forever for him to find the Greenville Hyatt but now that he was here he could attend the Sentinel meeting. We did not tell Ron that he was terribly off course and he was in the Lowe Hotel.

We stood up to go to the 5K awards ceremony. Ron stood and said, "Well, I guess it's time to go to the meeting," to which we replied that we were not going to the meeting but to the 5K awards ceremony. Ron never noticed that we were wearing sweaty running clothes, which should have tipped him off that we were not Sentinels.

The 5K awards ceremony was held outside the front entrance of the Lowe. While the ceremony was going on, Ron left the Lowe Hotel, portfolio in hand, and walked across the street. He tried to open the doors of the Mothman Museum with no luck. Spotting a person at a side door he rushed over and asked if the meetings were going to begin soon. It was explained to Ron that this was a museum and that no meetings were planned.

Ron returned to the lobby of the Lowe Hotel and began to review all of his paperwork for the Sentinel event. The confusion began to clear and Ron realized that he was in the wrong town and wrong state. At the desk, he discussed his plans with Ruth Finley to return back to his home in Indiana. Realizing he was over 350 miles from Greenville, he had decided it would be fruitless to carry on, and the return home was his best option. Ron checked out.

But he did not immediately leave town. Later in the day, Ro entered the hotel and saw him sitting in the lobby, talking on his cell phone with a file folder on his lap. She overheard him say he now knew how to get to the Greenville Hyatt.

After that, Ron disappeared from Point Pleasant.

Ron's story is similar to the character John Klein from the movie *The Mothman Prophecies*. John, a newspaper columnist, leaves work to drive home and ends up in Point Pleasant, hundreds of miles from home, and has to check into the Lowe Hotel. Ron also ends up in Point Pleasant very confused about how he ended up there. Ron's mind has trouble resolving this conundrum and floats between thinking he is in Greenville, SC, or very far away from his destination. His lucidity comes back on Saturday morning when he is forced to realize that the only event happening around him is the Mothman Festival.

It makes one wonder if this type of time and space displacement event may occur more often than we know, or if it is a harbinger of things to come.

Commentary

Is it possible to set out on a road for a destination and wind up somewhere else without knowing how you got there? And have missing time to boot? Such things do happen – they are documented in paranormal literature. Some displacements happen repeatedly in certain areas, as though a road goes through some dimensional warp, perhaps caused by the geography and energy of the land. Not every traveler gets caught in the warp. Why some do is a mystery. Other displacements occur without explanation.

Point Pleasant has more than its share of paranormal phenomena, including apparitions, doppelgängers, UFOs, mysterious creatures, and more. Although Ron's displacement started well before he arrived in Point Pleasant, it was an odd synchronicity with the timing of the Mothman Festival, an event that celebrates one of the strangest outbreaks of paranormal and UFO activity in the country.

Even odder, Ron could not seem to realize that he was not in the right place for his event. He kept looking for it, even though he was told he was in the wrong location. He disappeared as mysteriously as he appeared. Hopefully, he found his way back home.

THE OTHERWORLDLY EMERALD ISLE
Cynthia DeFay

A woman has a variety of strange experiences
on a trip to her ancestral home.

I have family ancestry and friends in Ireland, and I have always felt drawn to go there. In 2000, my husband, daughter, and I made the trip. It was the millennium year, and we were there for the summer solstice, which was a very powerful time. I had experiences that I can't explain.

Dreams of stones
There are ancient stone circles all over Ireland. The largest stone circle is in Limerick County, in a little place called Lough Gore, which means "the lake." I had been having serial dreams about stones telling me to go there. I knew I had to find them, and we did on the summer solstice itself. But getting there was no easy chore. Everywhere we went I had to ask, "Do you know where I can find the stone circle?"

Finally, we found Lough Gore. From the moment I walked inside the stone circle, I knew that this was the place my dreams were telling me about. I started crying and laughing uncontrollably at the same time. For some strange reason, I felt compelled to lie down in the center of that circle, with my face down and my arms splayed out, prone to the ground. I felt big energy waves coursing up through the earth and into my body. It was amazing, wave after wave after wave.

Weird glow and a mystery cow
Then I was directed by an impression that I had to go to yet another circle. It was behind a gate. We had to climb a fence to get into a field to where that circle was. My daughter, husband, and I all stood together on one of the stones. While there, I framed a little window with my fingers for a photo. When I looked through it, and was looking at my daughter, she had this odd yellow-green glow about her, which flickered rapidly and repeatedly, as if it were an x-ray, or something like that. It was really fast – on-off, on-off.

When I pulled my fingers away to collapse the frame, there was a cow standing right next to her, which wasn't there at all when I first framed her in my fingers to take the photo! We had not seen any cows at all – just sheep. Very strange indeed!

A portal on the Hill of Tara
We also went to the Hill of Tara, which was the social, political, and spiritual epicenter of Ireland in ancient agrarian times. It was the domain of the High King of Kings. There was an old ring-fort with three grass hills and gullies that you had go through to get to the top, where you had a view of three counties. At the very top was a tall standing stone called *Lia Fáil*, which means the "Stone of Destiny." According to Irish lore, it was one of the gifts that the *Tuatha Dé Danann* (which means the Tribe, or children, of the goddess Danu), the spirit race of Ireland, brought with them to this region. The *Tuatha Dé Danann* were the gods who dwelt in the Otherworld.

The Stone of Destiny reputedly had magical powers. It was on that hill for a significant reason. When the High King was to be chosen, he put his feet or hands on the stone. If he was the true High King, the stone screamed in joy. The stone also was said to have rejuvenating powers for the king.

It was eerie being there; you could feel an ancient power that was still present.

There is an area on the hill called "the Royal Seat." I walked clockwise around it three times and then walked into the center. When I went into the center, all of a sudden it was foggy. I couldn't see anything. I wasn't certain how much time passed. Then I heard a disembodied voice say, "It's been a long time since you've been here."

Actually, it was more like hundreds of voices speaking in unison – but strangely, it was seemingly all only one voice! It makes my skin all goose pimples again just talking about it. The voices said that it was a long time since they had seen me, and they were glad that I was "back home!"

I wondered what they meant. Had I been there in a past life? Or perhaps a parallel time?

I said to the voices, "Oh, wait a moment. I need to get back to my family, because they're probably looking for me." I was very thankful for being there, so I added, "And thank you for talking to me and connecting with me."

Then the strangest thing happened: A black bird feather fell through the mist and landed right at my feet. I bent over and picked it up and said, "Thank you."

I walked back around to the edge of the Royal Seat site, walked counterclockwise three times, and then walked out. Suddenly, it was clear again – no fog, no mist, nothing.

I heard my daughter say, "There you are, mommy! We've been looking for you for the past hour. Where have you gone?"

I couldn't believe it. She insisted I had been gone for an hour, but it only felt like minutes to me. Even stranger, none of my family saw the fog that surrounded me. They didn't see any physical change in the space that we were in.

I wondered if I had stepped into a time slip or portal.

My husband commented that they just suddenly noticed I was gone. We were all enjoying the lay of the land, going up and down the hills. They assumed I was off somewhere.

Missing time at Castle Matrix

A friend of ours, Liz Forrest O'Driscoll, put us up at her famed Castle Matrix in Rathkeale, which is near Shannon. The castle is old and

Norman, built in the thirteenth century. A lot of interesting things happened to us there. I suspect we slipped into and out of a lot of little time portals.

For instance, one morning we were upstairs in our room. We got up and readied for the day, which only took – it seemed – 10 or 20 minutes, or so. But when we went downstairs, we discovered a full two hours had elapsed!

Now, Ireland has its own energy patterns, and everything there feels slowed down. But the experience was unexplainable. The reality was, we were only 20 minutes at the most getting ready, and we went straight downstairs to find out two hours had passed, not 20 minutes. If that was not enough, we had another missing time experience while we ate our breakfast. It was a fast meal, just cereal and coffee, and then we washed our dishes and returned upstairs. To us, it felt like only another 20 minutes, but again, it turned out to be another two hours!

We went, *What the heck!*

I thought perhaps there was a portal of some kind, and vibrations that were specific to that place. Maybe it was me – I've been told I'm my own walking portal!

Strange photos and ghosts

On one occasion, Liz and I were sitting and talking in one of the rooms up in the tower of the castle. Liz wanted to show me a photo, but I was distracted by cold spots I could feel in parts of the room. When I put my hand out, it felt like it went through something tangible but invisible. Whatever was going on in that room, they could not keep the Internet, telephone, or TV reception in working order.

Then I looked at the photo. It was a black and white picture of a television screen in one of the rooms downstairs. There were images on the screen, but they looked overexposed.

Liz said, "Well, you're sensitive to these kinds of things. Will you hold it and tell me if you get a read off it?"

I held it up and looked at it and moved my hands over it. I started connecting with it. The photo undoubtedly was of someone associated with the castle's history in some way. It had a face of a bearded man wearing a turtleneck. He looked quite old.

Liz showed me a second similar photo of another man who had almost like a lion's mane for a beard. In one corner of the picture was a small child.

But, here's the rub: The TV was not on when the pictures were taken! How did these images show up on the screen when the TV was off? And who were they?

People did see spirits in the castle. Some other friends of ours who lived in County Cork told us that their sister had passed away in the castle, up in the library, and that her ghost visited often.

Newgrange: The eyes have it

We visited Newgrange, a famous prehistoric monument on the north side of the River Boyne in County Meath, Ireland. It is within the Neolithic *Brú na Bóinne* complex, which is part of the UNESCO World Heritage Site.

Newgrange is a passage tomb that includes *cairnes*, ceremonial piles of sacred stones. It was considered a portal that opened to the Otherworld, where the spirit race, the *Tuatha Dé Danann*, took up permanent residence after death. Newgrange has been carbon dated and determined to be even older than the oldest Egyptian pyramid.

As you go inside, there's a narrow stone structure with stone slabs on either side. If you are a tall or a large person, it can be difficult to move about inside. As you walk down the passage, it opens into three areas that are almost in the shape of a clover. Symbols and sigils are carved into the walls. Giant stone bowls are in the north, east, and west corners. The cremated remains of people were once placed in them. The passageway is aligned with the winter solstice, so that the light from the sun shines down through that tunnel and lights up the interior, on that one day only.

The tour guides showed us what the chamber would look like during the solstice. They turned all the lights off, making it pitch dark. I saw little silver orbs flying in and around my head. I piped up, "Oh, honey, are you seeing this? Isn't this cool?"

I put my arm on someone I thought was my husband, but it was not him! It was somebody else, who replied, "I don't know what you're talking about."

I was horribly embarrassed and said, "Oh, I'm sorry. It must've been something in my eye."

When the lights came back on, the chamber was lit up like the solstice, and all the symbols and carvings on the walls were lit up as well.

Download in the faery mound

We visited friends who owned 13 acres in the Castlepook in Doneraile. An old faery mound was on the property down by the river. Faery mounds are entrances to the faery underworld. In folklore, if you went down a faery mound, especially without permission, you never came back, but became trapped forever in faery land. Well, people could go down this one and come back – but they had unusual experiences while being underground.

The faery mound led to a tiny underground chamber just big enough for two people to sit cross-legged, shoulder to shoulder. People said they had profound experiences in there, sitting in the dark. I wanted to go inside it, but I was afraid. You had to get on your belly and slide down into it.

It took me a couple of days to muster up enough courage to do it. So, I did it as if it were a very sacred thing: I cleansed myself in a little river and then went in naked. I laid down on the downs and goatskins, which were very comfortable. It wasn't completely dark like Newgrange, because light came in through the small opening. My husband, Barth, came in for a while. We lit a candle.

I set an intention: *I'm going to let go of all the trauma from childhood, all the injuries to my sight. I'm going to dump it all into the earth and let the Earth Mother just receive that energy and transmute it into energy that everybody else can use.*

I felt like I had a major download. I thought I was in there for maybe an hour or so, but it turned out to be all day long!

I wore glasses, including sunglasses, to correct my vision, and I had taken my glasses off inside the chamber. When I came out, I put my regular glasses back on, and I couldn't see – everything was oddly out of focus. I took them off, rubbed them clean, and then put them back on again. I still couldn't see. Took them off, I could see; put them on, I could not see! For 10 years after that I did not need to wear corrective glasses! I had asked for all the injuries to my sight to be removed, and they were!

Meanwhile, something strange happened to my friends back at their house. They had the worst words they had had with each other in 30 years. The food had spoiled and the goat had gone dry. They blamed it all on me! They said that there were crystals underground at the faery mound, and while I had been inside having my experience, I supposedly diverted the energy that normally went out across the whole 13 acres.

An orb farewell
My trip to Ireland was one of the strangest trips I have ever taken. When we left on the airplane home, I saw those same little silver orbs that I had seen in Newgrange, flying around outside my airplane window. It was like Ireland itself was bidding me "good bye."

Commentary
It is not unusual for a traveler to have a range of unusual and paranormal experiences while visiting an exotic land. Some of them are subtle and some are dramatic, and combined they provide evidence to a person that they have temporarily stepped into an alternate reality. This is especially true when there is an ancestral connection. The land is partially energized by the "blood and bones" of living things that have passed into the earth. An energetic and familiar connection can be felt by psychically sensitive persons when they physically travel to certain places. The connections may be either generational or past life. In some cases, such as Cynthia's, it may be both.

Let's look at her experiences:

Dreams: *Cynthia experienced repeating dreams that she felt were calling her to visit certain areas, especially the standing stone circle at Lough Gore. This is a common experience, especially when people are visiting an ancestral homeland, or a place where they may have had a past life. If the person follows the dreams, they experience a profound spiritual and emotional connection with the place, such as the waves of energy that Cynthia felt rushing through her body, the extreme reaction of prostration, laughing, and crying, and the sense that she was "home." Such experiences may awaken other connections, and predispose individuals to having more unusual, even psychic, experiences.*

The glow: *It is not unusual to perceive odd lights and glows in highly energized places, and such may have been the case with the glow around Cynthia's daughter.*

Cow: *The sudden appearance of the cow is less likely to be paranormal in nature. Cynthia and Barth said they saw no cows around, only sheep. However, when attention is diverted and focused on other things, such as landscapes and monuments, a person may fail to notice things in the background. This has been demonstrated in experiments. One of the most famous is the "gorilla film," in which viewers are asked to watch the exchanges of a basketball while a game is played on a court. Few people notice that a man in a gorilla suit walks onto the court and starts playing with the others.*

Nonetheless, we can't dismiss the cow incident as having no meaning. It was an odd synchronicity for Cynthia, and at the least underscored the feeling that she was in some alternate reality.

The Hill of Tara: *Cynthia's experience of a sudden fog and then missing time is another alternate reality experience, especially at sacred sites. Time slips into alternate realities are often accompanied by marked changes in the environment. There are sudden fogs and mists that obscure surroundings. Sometimes the percipient notices that the environment shifts to a "weird" sensation, with a heaviness in the air and the cessation of all noise, including nature. Surroundings, if they are visible, may look distorted. Such experiences have been well documented in paranormal literature.*

Are portals created by land energy? Ancient sacred sites are often located at places where the energy of the land is intensified by ley lines and magnetic anomalies. These energies may affect the brain and consciousness, opening a portal to an alternate reality that is always present, but usually beyond the ken of waking consciousness.

The perceptions of the experiencer vary. Some feel taken back in time, and some feel as though they have stepped into a parallel reality. Cynthia seemed to connect with her ancestral past and possibly a past life, with the voices that said it had been a long time since she had been there – even though in this life, she had never been there before.

In shifts to altered states and realities, time passes much differently. Individuals often experience missing time – they feel a short period has elapsed when hours have passed. (This is a characteristic of entity encounters as well, and the abduction and contact experiences described in UFO literature.)

Cynthia may have initiated this shift herself and literally opened the portal door by the ritual she did: walking three times clockwise around the Royal Seat. This is a movement called deosil, *and is used in magical ritual to mark and set a protected sacred space. The space within becomes a portal for interaction with the spirit realm. The sacred space is taken down by walking the circle counterclockwise, called* widdershins. *When Cynthia did that three times, the sacred space/alternate reality was broken and she returned to "normal" space. (We do not know if Cynthia knew to do this, or did this spontaneously.)*

The appearance of the bird feather is a common phenomenon as well. Such feathers seem to materialize out of the air and float down to the experiencer. They are taken as signs from the spirit world and validation of experiences. White ones are usually interpreted as signs from angels and the dead. Black ones are omens of gods and power, and have a connection to the dead, too.

Ireland is a land where the Otherworld – the land of the dead, faeries, and the gods – is still potent and accessible. Interestingly, the raven and crow are totems of The Morrigan, the powerful Triple Goddess of Irish lore.

Missing time at the castle: *The time displacements at Castle Matrix are harder to explain as paranormal incidents, even though the castle seems to have housed odd energies (cold spots and rooms where equipment and technology malfunctioned). Cynthia commented that life in Ireland moves slowly, and so these experiences could simply have been adjustments to a slower pace of life than she and her family considered "normal." They probably were still recalibrating the time that was spent on various activities. They also might not have paid as much attention to watches and clocks as usual. It "seemed" to them that only a few minutes had passed, but that may not have been the case.*

On the other hand, Cynthia had already had episodes of being plunged into alternate realities, where the passage of time is distorted.

Thus, her entire stay in Ireland could have been tinged with the feeling that she was visiting an "Elsewhere."

TV screen photos: *The appearance of anomalous images on dark screens, such as televisions and computers that have been turned off, is a documented paranormal phenomenon. Liz's photos seem to have captured residual energy, the ghostly imprints of people who perhaps had occupied the castle in times past. Why such images manifest, and under what conditions, remains unknown. Sometimes it appears that a person with the right energy, such as a psychic or medium, serves as a catalyst for the energy needed to make images manifest. Cynthia acknowledged that she had psychic gifts, although she apparently had not developed them much.*

In certain avenues of research to communicate with the dead and spirits, called Instrumental Transcommunication (ITC), dark television and computers screens are used as blank slates for the possible transmission of images of faces and places from the Other Side. Remarkable images have been captured since the 1970s.

Silver orbs at Newgrange and on the airplane: *These are natural phenomena, caused by adjustments of the eye. They are especially common when lights are suddenly turned off and an environment becomes pitch dark, and when looking at a bright blue background, such as gazing out an airplane window into the sky. The extent of them varies significantly by individual.*

Changes in vision at the faery mound: *Cynthia said she experienced a "download" while inside the faery mound, but provided few details beyond the intention she set. A "download" is a term to describe an experience of receiving a rush of information and insights – it is a big inspiration. Many people credit downloads to spirits and aliens, because they seem to originate from outside the individual. Some report profound physical sensations and changes as well.*

The interesting aspect of the change in her vision – a healing she requested in her intention – is that faeries are renowned for altering vision in people. Most commonly, they grant "second sight," or clairvoyance, to people – and they also take it away if a person displeases them. *They have been reported to strike people blind. Thus, it is within the realm of possibility that the faeries – or the peculiar energies of the faery mound – had a physical effect upon Cynthia's vision. This seems to have temporarily consumed the subtle energy of the land, judging from the experiences of her friends back at the house. We can assume their observations are sound, for as longtime residents of the land, they would be quite familiar with its energy.*

Other than the change in her vision, which lasted for a decade, Cynthia did not say whether she was permanently altered in other ways by her experiences (such as an increase in clairvoyance and psychic events), or whether the effects subsided upon returning home. We can speculate that it may have been a bit of both.

THE ROBIN HOOD WINK
Robert Svihus

An unexpected side trip turns into a twilight zone for two travelers.

This story is about Robin Hood. My wife and I were traveling in England, and wound up going to Robin Hood country in Nottingham, a city we originally had no intentions to visit. It just happened in an odd sort of way – and so did the rest of our little side trip.

We were driving down a highway about 40 miles outside of Nottingham, planning to bypass the city. I think we got turned around at a confusing traffic circle. We stopped at a signal, and my wife, Eva, said, "What am I going to do?"

"I don't know," I answered.

Just then, a little man came up in a car right alongside of us. He had a big handlebar mustache and a little jaunty cap with a feather in it. My wife looked at him, and he gave us a big wink.

We nodded to him, and he nodded back. He said, "Well, follow me." Evidently, he sensed that we didn't know how to get around this roundabout.

Eva thought that he meant literally to follow him, so, instead of going around the roundabout, we followed him all the way into Nottingham.

That's how we got to see Robin Hood.

We decided to stay and checked into a beautiful hotel in town, all stainless steel, and each bed had its own radio and its own television. It was gorgeous.

Right down the street were a big, old museum and castle. We decided to visit them. A guide who took us through the castle said it went back to the time of the Druids. It had underground passageways that he opened for us, and a dungeon where people were tossed during the time of Robin Hood, in the 1600s.

The guide said people had experienced many ghosts in the castle. "The ghosts come out of the kitchen every night and make bells ring, and a green light goes up the old hand-carved stairway," he told us. "We usually don't allow anybody in here anymore, because people have become frightened, and have fallen off the stairway into the big holes down there in the dungeon. The holes are full of water, and when people died of plague and other diseases, their bodies would be thrown there. 'Bottomless pits,' they called them. Skeletons are still found there because the water has lime in it, and is a preservative."

As you can imagine, we quickly got out of there. We decided to go around the outside of the castle. We descended a narrow stairway to the outside of the castle to the moat, which was full of water. The guide told us about sieges that had taken place there. As we walked along the centuries-old pathways, it felt like we were going back in time.

I came upon a statue of Robin Hood, kneeling with a bow pulled back ready to shoot. It was a gorgeous statue made of bronze. He had a sardonic smile on his face, and if you looked at him a certain way, it seemed like he was alive. It was almost uncanny.

I went right up to him and looked at him, and started taking photographs. It was slightly cloudy that day, but rays of the sun hit the statue at different spots. One sun ray just happened to hit Robin Hood right smack in the eye, and I swear to God, *he winked at me!*

A bronze Robin Hood statue comes to life in Nottingham, England. Credit: John Weaver.

I did a double-take and looked around in complete disbelief. I thought I was seeing things.

I looked at him again and said, "Holy Jesus!"

I swear to God he winked at me! I'm no dummy – I've got newsmaker awards for writing. I'm a level-headed guy, and a scientist as well. I don't believe in such things, but I was so sure that he winked at me, I even got a little chill over me.

I looked around to see if my wife (or anyone) was looking – you know, as a kind of a reality check. I looked back at Robin Hood again and took a photo. I said, "Oh God!" I just couldn't fathom what had happened. I was in complete disbelief!

My wife had gone ahead of me, and now she looked back and said, "Well, come on."

I was about to go – and I'll be doggone – I couldn't move my left foot. So help me God, I could *not* move my left foot! The reason was my shoelace had come undone. I apparently stepped on my shoelace just as I went to move, and I became frozen in place. I just could *not* move my foot!

I was really disturbed over this. It threw me for a loop, because – *my God* – Robin Hood had not only winked at me, I was now paralyzed, and I couldn't move!

Panic set in. Here I was, a perfectly level-headed guy. I don't believe in anything but real scientific things, and I was sweating over this.

I knelt to tie my laces, and suddenly saw, right on the border of the walk in the black mud, a gray, round piece, about the size of an American quarter, just staring at me. It was round and sort of smashed in on one side with a little hollow in it.

I looked at the thing and picked it up. It was a piece of lead. It looked like it had come out of an old blunderbuss gun. It must have been there for hundreds of years! If I hadn't stooped to tie my laces, I would never have found that piece.

I took it to the curator at the museum and showed him what I found.

He said, "Oh, that shot is very ancient. There was a siege here at one time, and there were a lot of blunderbuss guns shooting, and lead being thrown around. Evidently the gardeners dug it up." He estimated that it was about 400 years old.

I offered it to him. "Put it in the museum."

"No," he said. "It's for you. It was meant for you. "If you hadn't done what you did, you'd never have found that piece. You take it home."

I took the lead piece home, an amazing souvenir that I acquired because Robin Hood winked at me, my laces were untied, and I couldn't move my feet. What are the odds?

I still think about the wink. I will never forget it. Common sense says it could not have happened, but it did, it was real. Robin Hood winked! And that souvenir was indeed meant for me.

Commentary

Can a bronze statue really wink? Assuming this was not a trick of light playing on metal, the winking Robin Hood is related to cases of religious statues that manifest physical phenomena, such as statues that weep watery or bloody tears. One might argue that the religious statues fall into the category of miracles, and a winking bronze statue of an outlaw does not, but the bottom line is, an inanimate statue exhibits animation. A winking Robin Hood statue certainly falls within the realm of paranormal possibility.

Even more curious is the odd little fellow who mysteriously appeared at a crucial moment and led the couple into their adventure. Small, jaunty, and wearing a feather in his cap, he is more like a faery than a person. He led them astray – just as faeries are wont to do. And he winked!

Robert may think that the blunderbuss shot was the purpose of the adventure – but perhaps the purpose was simply the adventure itself, a short excursion into a mind-bending twilight zone.

THE SOUNDS OF STONEHENGE
Veronica Appolonia

Mystical experiences at an ancient site are life-transforming
for a young woman.

In 2002, I took my first trip to England, on a tour. The organizer arranged for us to have a private hour inside Stonehenge among the stones before it opened to the public. The site was not fenced off then, and people could wander around outside the stones during public hours, and go inside the stones by appointment off hours. I'd always dreamed of going there – it looked like such a powerful place.

I walked down a little paved pathway from the visitor center to the stones. As I got closer, I could feel power and energy ripple off them to the extent that I felt I was going be knocked flat if I approached too quickly. I slowed down.

I entered the stones and just stood there with tears running down my face. I was awash with this feeling of energy, slowly approaching and then being among the stones, and finally getting to touch them.

At one point, I stood between two of the smaller stones and put my hands on them. I imagined being one of the stones, and what it would be like to have been there all those thousands of years. I found myself wishing that I knew the secrets that they had to tell.

It was a powerful experience that had a deep impact on me. When I came back home, I knew I needed to be doing something other than what I was doing, which was working in the corporate world. I knew that was not the path I was supposed to take. It was almost like an itch under the skin.

I went my second time to England and Stonehenge the next year, in 2003. Again, we got an opportunity to visit the stones before the site was open to the public. I could still feel the power, but I knew I wasn't going get knocked flat, so I approached with more confidence.

It had rained the night before, and in some pockets of the stones there were little pools of water. Having been raised Catholic (I'm not Catholic anymore), I had this desire to anoint myself with the water resting in the stones.

I touched my throat with this water. Then I went around and touched every stone, laying my hands on them. Then I sat for a while and let myself be open to thoughts and feelings.

Then a peculiar thing happened. I found myself sensing the music, the vibrations, that were in the stones, and I started humming what I thought I was hearing from the stones. It was akin to a conversation. I felt a tremendous urge to start writing songs.

Up until that trip to England, I had never written a song in my life. I sang in a choir called Sacred Fire, and after the visit to Stonehenge we were performing at a Goddess Conference in Glastonbury. Toward the end of that trip, I wrote my first chant, called "There is no time but now," and it came about as I was sitting in the Chalice Well Gardens in Glastonbury. I didn't want to go back to the States, because I had a job there that I just absolutely loathed. The stress was horrible.

I was sitting there at the well thinking about how I didn't want to go back, and I only had a few days left. I was starting to stress myself out. I had to pause and remind myself that "there is no time but now" and "there is no place but here" to bring myself back to the moment – to not worry about what was going happen a few days from then, so as not to spoil the beauty in those Chalice Well Gardens by stressing myself out over a job I hated. I kept repeating that to myself, and it ended up being a chant. It has four lines sung as a round:

> There is no time but now,
> There is no place but here.
> In the Sacred we do stand
> In a circle hand in hand.

By the time I got home, songs just started coming to me. I wrote another song a couple of days after we got back. I went to choir rehearsal. On my way home, I was thinking I would have to go back to work the next day, and all the wonderful joy I had from the trip just drained away from me.

While I was driving, I kept thinking, *Don't let them steal your power, don't let them take it away,* and *Don't hand it to them on a silver plate cause if you do you'll pay.* By the time I got home I had another song.

I quit that job. I wrote yet another new song on the day that I gave my notice, because I was so happy. It's called "Learn how to fly." It's a blues song.

My visits to Stonehenge changed my life in many ways. I moved into a body, song, and healing arts center, and then took over the property management of it. My choir published a book of original songs by members, and I contributed several, which have been performed in concerts. They were all inspired by my visits to Stonehenge.

Commentary
Travel to exotic places – and especially sacred sites such as Stonehenge – often lead to a dramatic change or breakthrough. The seeds for change have already been sewn, and an experience or string of experiences can help them sprout and bloom. A person might have sudden and intense clarity and courage for letting go of the old and embracing the new, whether it's a relationship or a job. In Veronica's case, she was already disaffected by her job. Evidently, she had an undeveloped talent for music and song, which the breakthrough energy brought to the surface.

The mystical sounds of Stonehenge are legendary. Many visitors, awed by the size, age, and mystery of these ancient stones, feel they have stories to tell. Natural stone is one of the best materials for psychometry, the sensing of impressions of the past via the touching and handling of objects. People place their hands on the stones to make an energetic and psychic connection, and many of them "hear" words or conversations, impressions about what the stones themselves have to say.

Stonehenge is still shrouded in mystery. It was built first as an earthwork henge around 3100 BCE by a culture that left no written records, and was modified up to about 1600 BCE. The present stones were erected around 2500 BCE. Many theories, some fanciful, have been put forward for centuries as to the builders and their purposes. Stonehenge has been linked to healing, sacrifice, the Druids, King Arthur, and even extraterrestrials. Only the stones know the truth.

The circle is now fenced off and visitors walk around them on a viewing path. Small groups and tours can arrange to visit inside the stones before and after hours.

From mystical and psychic perspectives, the energy of sacred sites can affect consciousness. Sacred sites often sit on unusual land, such as ley line areas or magnetic anomalies. These factors, coupled with long histories of activity – which leave buildups of residual energy – can facilitate creative and spiritual breakthroughs for visitors. It is not unusual for people to feel intense emotions, such as euphoria, weeping, and expansiveness, as though being in that place brings one closer to something sacred and divine.

According to dowsing experts, Stonehenge is at the hub of a network of 14 lines, making it a powerful "portal" where dimensions and time are fluid. Veronica, poised for change, tapped into that energy and allowed it to carry her into transformation.

STREETLIGHTS THAT GO BLINK IN THE NIGHT
Michael Brein

Can an individual cause street lights to go off and on?

W hen strange events occur, it is one thing; when the same weird events occur repeatedly, well... do not let anyone tell you that it's all in your imagination. And when you have a lifetime of unusual events, the recurrence of an anomaly is something you notice.

The Inner Psychic in me duly notes the variety of such paranormal happenings over my life, accepts them, and sometimes even fears them. But I must admit: I am totally perplexed by one of the strangest of them all in my life – the darn streetlights that blink out in the night when I'm near them!

It comes and goes in phases. Sometimes a single light will blink out. One of these isolated events happened while I was walking with a friend of mine from a Thai restaurant in Honolulu to a nearby supermarket.

"Jack, you see that light?" I said spontaneously to my friend. "It's going to blink out when we come under it." And it did! When we bought our beer and headed back to the restaurant, I said, "Now it will come back on." And it did, just as we passed under it. I knew it would happen, instantly, with immediacy, and without thinking about it.

Campus lights blinked out on a series of Monday and Wednesday nights when I was on my way to a class I taught. These were barely above my head. On one sequence of three nights, three lights blinked out in a row on these nights. It was never the same lights, either, so I could not automatically assume they were near the end of their life and about to go out.

Once, a whole block of city lights wigged out just as I zoomed past in my car.

Many, many streetlights would do the same as I passed under them on the freeways, alleyways, and small streets. This happened so often that I became convinced that it must have had something to do with me.

So, it was no surprise when I was dining one evening on the second floor of a restaurant in Cozumel, Mexico, when a streetlight just outside the window and level with me suddenly blinked out! This was the first and only time in my travels that a streetlight paid homage to the Inner Psychic in me. I recall smiling and acknowledging to myself that this was just one more possible anomalous event in my life. Of course, it might just be a bad or tricky streetlight. After all, this was Mexico, and anything could happen!

I found a possible explanation of what was happening to me. Hilary Evans, a writer on anomalous subjects, once did an informal study on what he called "the Streetlight Interference Phenomenon (SLI)." He noticed that many people report similar happenings with streetlights. In his study, he found that people who reported streetlights blinking out on them also tended to have other synchronicity events as well.

I've had many odd synchronicity experiences, so maybe there is something to this SLI after all. The Inner Psychic in me accepts this as one among many paranormal events in my life.

Commentary

The Street Light Interference (SLI) effect documented by Hilary Evans is controversial. Skeptics dismiss SLI as an illusion caused by the natural life cycles of high pressure sodium street lights, in which they blink on and off more frequently as they near their end. Skeptics also point to the fact that SLI has never been documented scientifically, due to the inability of subjects to make streetlights go on and off at will. It seems to be an arbitrary and puzzling phenomenon.

Though SLI has never been debunked, it has not been explained satisfactorily, either.

In his book Sliders: The Enigma of Streetlight Interference *(2011), Evans presents case histories and explains why they cannot be explained easily, such as due to illusion, coincidence, mechanical malfunctions, tricks of light, and so on. Evans notes that experiencers are often in an altered state, including being happy and distracted, though there is no definable consistency.*

Interestingly, SLI-prone people also seem to have unusual effects on batteries and electricity: watches and clocks stop working, electrical lights and appliances don't work right, computers malfunction. These effects also occur in certain cases of spontaneous human-generated psychokinesis (mind over matter) that fall into "poltergeist" categories. Such cases suggest that certain individuals may have natural energy – perhaps subtle energy – that has an adverse effect on electromagnetic and electrical fields. This subtle energy may also be at work in synchronicity, and the frequency of paranormal phenomena.

MYSTERIOUS PEOPLE, SPIRITS, AND BEINGS

I AM NOT ALONE
Joe Mullins

*A World War II soldier discovers he is not the only presence
on an island jungle – and the "Other" is not human.*

In May or June of 1942, I landed on an isolated Polynesian island called Uvea (now called Wallis & Futuna), which was about 300 miles west of Samoa and 300 miles north of Fiji. I was sent up into the interior in the hills and was stationed beside a crater lake in the depths of the rain forest. The crater lake was most unusual. It had straight down, circular walls that descended for about 200 feet. It was about three-quarters of a mile across, shaped in almost a perfect circle. The whole place had a look like Arthur Conan Doyle's *Lost World.*

The jungle – a heavy rain forest – sat on top of the cliffs and hung over them. No Polynesian natives went there often, so I was mostly alone in this place. It had an air of spookiness. I used to think, when I'd sit out looking over the crater lake and the sheer walls with the jungle on top, *God, the only thing lacking is a dinosaur.*

At night, I had to stand guard in a little area away from the lake shore. I constantly had the feeling that there was a brooding presence hovering over me. Not a man, not a woman, but an 'it-like' presence hanging over this area of the island at night.

It was so tangible that I could almost feel it, and my hair would stand straight up. It was frightening, but in a rich sort of way.

I thought of Paul Caponigro, a world-famous photographer at the time, who spoke about similar presences, which he had experienced in the countryside of western Ireland, and at the volcano on the Big Island of Hawaii. He described the presences as either hovering or innate in the land itself.

I felt the presence for the whole time I was on that island. It never "spoke" to me, and I never felt threatened by it, but I knew that it was powerful, and that if I should ever displease it, I would be in for trouble.

Commentary
Joe might have experienced a guardian of the land, a type of ancient spirit or indwelling presence described in many cultures by various names. The Romans called such a spirit a "genius," which means an attendant spirit, usually to a place or a person. The genii were like minor gods, assigned to places such as lakes, forests, and glens, whose duty it was to protect the land from harm. They also were attached to cities, homes, buildings – anything that needed protection from evil spirits and harmful humans. They had either a masculine or feminine presence. In Hawaii, Madame Pele, the goddess of volcanoes, functions in the same way as a protector. Guardians of places are renowned for wreaking vengeance upon humans who displease them by failing to properly respect the land.

Land guardian spirits are found around the world, particularly in cultures where beliefs in animism – the indwelling presence of Spirit – are strong. When sensed, they are usually a brooding, undefined presence. They can convey power and intent. They do not interfere with people unless some boundary of theirs is violated. In Polynesian mythology, everything is imbued with a sacred power called mana, *which carries all sorts of taboos. Violating the taboos results in great misfortune such as illness and even death.*

The spread of civilization, with the clearing of land and building upon it, has weakened and destroyed much of the land guardian presence. It can still be felt in remote areas, as Joe experienced on that remote part of the island.

THE CANE
Monica Osborne

A life lesson is learned from a mysterious old man.

How is it that we can be so blind about ourselves, yet, at the same time, see these self-same foibles so readily in others? Sometimes it takes a traumatic experience – and in this case a mystical occurrence in Morocco – to recognize our own shortcomings and deal with them. It is so easy to spot the weaknesses of others, while ignoring our own.

Harold, "Hal," a friend of ours, told us the story, which follows.

1

We were sitting on a bus one night. We had a cup of tea, and then Hal said to us, "I would like to share an experience with you. Would you like to listen to me?"

We nodded.

Hal began his story:

I was taking a walk with my friend Roger to a little village near Agadir, which we call the "banana village," because there are always bananas growing around the village, and the Moroccans sit in the street all day long, offering and selling nothing but bananas. We were walking along the street up to the end of the village, and we found that the street changed into a little path that seemed to lead into the mountains further away. We kept on walking and found ourselves alone after a while, walking uphill in the sunshine towards the mountains. We passed by thorn bushes and wild growing flowers. After two hours or three, we reached a peak. We looked for a place to rest, and discovered a little cave that seemed to suit perfectly to our purpose.

We sat down inside the shade protecting us from the sun, which had become very hot. The cave seemed to be made for just one person to live in. It had a fireplace in one corner. We couldn't make up our minds whether the cave had been made by nature or by man, but we immediately liked this place a lot, so we decided to stay there for a couple of days. We cooked tea at night on the fireplace and watched the stars.

After two days my friend seemed to become very ill, and we finally decided we had to leave this place. Roger felt more and more weak, so I had to bring him to the hospital in Agadir, where he was told he had hepatitis.

After Roger was taken care of, I decided I wanted to stay some more days in the cave in the mountain by myself, and I walked up there again.

2

One morning I was sitting there at the cave, and a Moroccan passed by with two mules. One little mule was heavily loaded with sacks and one big one didn't carry any load. The Moroccan was walking behind the mules guiding them with a little stick that he carried in his hand. When he saw me, he made a gesture inviting me to come along with him. I joined him and we walked together on this little path that was barely broad enough for one mule.

Communication seemed to be impossible, because we didn't speak each other's language, so I offered him a cigarette. He took it, and I could see from his face that he was happy to smoke the cigarette. We kept on walking slowly behind the mules, both of us smoking, and there seemed to be a perfect understanding between us.

From time to time he gestured at his mules trying to make me understand how dumb the little one was, which he hit with a stick whenever it stumbled and was slow at trying to make his way on this little path.

I wondered how it was possible that this Moroccan, who seemed to be so sensitive toward me and with whom I could share the joy of walking together through the nature, could be so insensitive towards another living being that was struggling under his load and getting hit by a stick. Why didn't he put some of the load on the bigger mule, which seemed to be much stronger and carried no load? I could not fathom answers to my questions.

Meanwhile, we had nearly reached the village. I thought that he lived there and that he intended to invite me to his house.

But, suddenly he stopped and gestured that this was the point where I had to leave him, making signs with his hands that I should walk away. I made, "Why?" and, "I would like to go on with you to your house."

After a while I understood that he didn't live in this village and that he had to go further on into the mountains, up and down the next mountain, far away from the village where he lived, and that this way would be too long for me.

So, we parted shaking hands. I walked slowly back again, still thinking about this man, to whom it seemed so natural to walk on foot the whole day with his mules, to get home again with a few belongings and the food his mule carried. He seemed to be so perfectly tuned in with nature that surrounded him every day, and he seemed happy with his life, and he had only what was necessary. But I still wondered why, in spite of his natural environment, from which he could learn so much about nature, was he still so insensitive towards his little mule?

3

I sat down in the grass and rolled a joint and slowly walked uphill, smoking. Suddenly I was startled by the untouched beauty around me and the peace that emerged from there. It gave me a feeling of floating that went back and forth between flowers and the grass and the road and myself.

Then my eyes spotted a figure sitting maybe 100 meters away. He was cross-legged, bending his body forward over something. He was all dressed in white.

I thought, *This doesn't seem to be realistic.* I slowly approached the figure from the side. As I came nearer, I recognized that it was an old man, whose hands were gently playing with something that I thought to be little stones.

As he heard my steps, he turned around and a big smile appeared on his face. I was pushing the thought away that this smiling old man, all dressed in white, totally alone in the middle of nature far away from other humans, could be but a vision. Mystical thoughts came to my mind.

Then I saw that the old man was reaching for something behind him. As I looked at it, I saw that he was holding a package of postcards. Still smiling at me, he told me to have a look. The cards showed photos of the town of Agadir and other tourist places in Morocco.

I thought, *Well, this is but an old man sitting here trying to make some business by selling postcards to tourists who pass by.*

Then I looked at the little things he had been playing with, and they seemed to be very old dried up almonds, dates, and nuts, all wrinkly and sad-looking.

Then I discovered the cane that lay by his side. It looked beautiful to me, curved at the end. It just seemed to me to be made for your hand and to walk with it. It seemed that it had been worked on carefully for a long time to make it smooth and perfect-looking.

I suddenly thought, *I want to have this cane! Why not offer him some money for it in trade?* I pointed to it and said, "I want to have this cane. Give me your cane and I give you two *dirham*."

The old man looked at me and looked at his cane and his smile vanished. He looked at me as if he didn't understand. I pointed to it again. "I want your cane, and I give you two *dirham*."

He shook his head, telling me that this was his cane and he couldn't sell it.

So, I just took the cane. I said, "I take your cane and I give you money." I showed him some money. He did not look at me and seemed to think. Then he suddenly stretched out his hand. I put the money in it and felt the cane in my possession.

He turned around and bent over his nuts, and never looked at me again. He gathered the nuts and the postcards and made an effort to get up. I could see that he had trouble getting to his feet without the help of his cane, and he was a little shaky, but he finally managed to stand up. He put one of the old, scrubby-looking dates in his mouth and began chewing it.

4

I turned around and walked away with the cane in my hand. It was suited perfectly to my hand, and it was a pleasure to walk with it. I had been walking for a few minutes when suddenly I realized I was walking with this old man's cane. Maybe he had worked it for many years and had had it for many years and had gotten attached to it. Maybe it would take him a long time to make another one as beautiful as this one. This was his cane. He had to walk with this cane. He needed this cane, and I traded it for some money.

I began to feel bad about it and decided I would give him his cane back. I went back to the place where I had met him, but he was gone. I thought, *I have to find him to give him his cane back. It's only a few minutes since I left him, and he cannot be far away. He cannot walk fast without his cane.*

I went in different directions trying to find him again, but wherever I looked, I could not see him. He had just disappeared.

I decided to go down to the village; maybe people knew him there and they could give him his cane back, or tell me where he lived.

I arrived in the village and asked different people, "Who is the old man that is all dressed in white and who has been sitting up on the hill with postcards? Where does he live? Here, I have his cane, and I want to give it back to him."

Nobody seemed to know him. They shook their heads, and I had to walk all the way back to my cave. I still had the cane. I felt that the cane had a big value for me.

5

In the evening a Moroccan came over to my cave. He had come from time to time to drink tea with me and Roger, and this night he came to sit with me near my fireplace.

While he was there, I had put the cane in a place where I could watch it all the time out of the silly fear that this friendly Moroccan might take it.

When he left, I wanted to go to sleep, but I had to hide my cane first. Above this cave there was another cave, and from the back corner of the first, a few steps went up to the second. Up there I had put a few belongings: my teapot, a gas stove, and some other things. Up there was a fireplace, too, and in the ashes I put my cane, well covering it with gray ash so that it looked like burnt or half-burned wood. What seemed important to me was, that whoever wanted to go upstairs had to pass through the cave I slept in, so I would wake up and hear them.

6

I went to bed and had a good sleep. In the early morning, I suddenly woke up from some noise. It sounded like scratching, and it was coming from upstairs. I was about to jump up when I thought, *If this is somebody that has gone upstairs to steal something from me, he has to come down again and pass by my sleeping place to leave the cave.*

There was no other way out, so I could catch him when he actually had committed the stealing, trying to walk out with whatever he stole. So I waited with nervous tension, and then I could hear slow steps coming down. I laid motionless, in my mind I was already seeing myself suddenly jump up and hold the thief.

Then I saw the old man slowly coming down the few narrow steps. He seemed to watch out not to fall down, for he had to bend over, because the wall was not high. I didn't see the cane.

I wondered how he had found out that I was staying in this cave. Nobody had followed me on my way back. And how did he know that there was another cave above?

Maybe it was he who had built this cave and it was his. Maybe he had worked for years to make a home out of it. Maybe... I did not know. But whatever might be the truth, he had come to look for his cane.

Maybe he had stolen something else, but I could prove it. Would I stop him right then, or would I let him walk out and then check?

I pretended to be asleep and let him leave. Then I jumped up and ran upstairs. I could see with one glance that none of my personal belongings had been stolen.

I kneeled down by the fireplace to see if the cane was still hidden under the ashes. I saw immediately that he had been searching with his hands for it, but I could make out the shape of the cane with my eyes.

I reached for it, and then I saw that it was another cane – just an ordinary cane that had been worked on with little care. *Oh, he has taken his cane and left me this crummy one,* I thought. Immediately it came to my mind: *I want my beautiful cane back. We made the deal, so it is mine. I did not pay for this old one that is not nearly comparable.*

7

I had to catch the old man and get my cane back. I ran down out of the cave and I saw he was not very far, walking away without hurrying. I caught him, and I could see he was carrying the real one. I told him, "You come back with me to the cave, and you take the other cane and give me mine. It is mine now."

He looked at me without saying a word and slowly walked back with me to the cave. I had the other cane leaning on the wall, took it and handed it over to him. "You take this one and give me the other one back. I gave you money for the cane you took from me."

Then something strange happened. He told me to sit down, and then he sat down, cross-legged. He moved his body back and forth rhythmically. He told me to do the same. This went on for a while, and then he started chanting a sing-sang. He invited me to sing with him, and so I did. We were both sitting there chanting together, and his voice was very soothing, and there was nothing else but we sitting and chanting together.

This went on for at least half an hour. Then he slowly ended the sing-sang. He got up, trying not to lose his balance without the help of the cane, and I could see him struggle again. He turned around, took his cane, slowly walked out of the cave, and walked away with his cane. He never turned around and I never saw him again.

8

I was left with the other, plain cane. Ever since then, I walk with it and take it with me wherever I can. I nearly lost it a couple of times. Once I forgot it in a restaurant. When I went back a few hours later, I found they had put the cane aside for me.

Another time it was collected by some people in my absence. They were looking for wood to make fire in the evening, and when I came the next morning my cane was lying with the firewood, but it was there. They had not burned it. So, I have always found it back.

This is the experience I wanted to share with you.

Commentary

Hal's story reveals a lesson about selfishness and insensitivity, with some unexplained elements bordering on the mystical. He is struck by the insensitivity of the mule-beating man, but it does not occur to him that he is just as insensitive to take away a cane that is obviously needed by its infirm and old owner. Because of its beauty, he covets it for himself. He experiences remorse, but quickly gets over it and goes to great lengths to hide the cane.

The old man is mysterious, disappearing too quickly after he and Hal part the first time. No one in the village admits to knowing who he is. There is no explanation for how he knew where Hal was staying – and that the cane would be hidden in a second cave above the first. It is possible that he had prior knowledge of the caves, as Hal thought. It may also have been possible for someone in the village to tell him about Hal, and it may have been generally known that Hal was staying in the cave. But how did an old man, shuffling along with a cane in the dark, make it up the mountain to the cave, and get past Hal to make it upstairs to the second cave?

The plain cane became attached to Hal in an uncanny way. He cannot seem to lose it. It is a constant reminder of his selfish behavior, and how an old man had to go to great lengths to get his beloved cane back.

Sometimes we are tested by the divine, who sends messengers in disguise to see whether we take the high road or the low road. Did Hal encounter an old man – or something else?

THE NULLARBOR NYMPH
B.B. Dupre

A desperate woman hitchhiking with her children is mistaken
for a supernatural being.

I n 1977, I emigrated from England to Australia with my three
children under a scheme called the Fairbridge Child Migration
Act. The government rounded up poor or orphaned children in
the U.K., and they also offered the plan to single mothers with sick
children. I was a single mother, 27 years old, and my kids were three,
five, and seven, and one of my daughters had asthma. I looked at
promotional films about the scheme and decided to do it. I was told I
would be a house mother with my children at the Fairbridge Society,
an Aborigine encampment in Pinjarra, 160 miles into the desert.

When we got to Australia, we found out that they wanted to
take my children away from me and send them to Perth until they

were 18. It was a nightmare. It was a disgusting scheme, which caused an uproar and was eventually outlawed and discontinued.

To keep my family together, I had to kidnap my children from the children's home and walk across Australia to escape to Sydney. We just ran. We were on the lam. We hitchhiked through the middle of the desert in the Nullarbor Plain, which is flat and treeless. The truck we were in broke down, and we then had to walk hundreds of miles. We had never been to Australia in our lives. We hadn't got water, anything. Me, three kids, no luggage, just the clothes on our backs.

Nobody stopped to help us – they just waved at us as they went by. I put a sheepskin rug around all of us with "SOS" written on it in giant letters, and they still wouldn't pick us up. I could not understand why.

It was so hot and horrible that we started hallucinating. It was 50 degrees Celsius (122 degrees Fahrenheit) and we had no water. Nothing at all. We had no idea how dangerous the situation was – we just knew we had to get Sydney. We all could have died out there.

Eventually someone picked up us and we got to Sydney. It took us three weeks. In an odd irony, Sydney was cold! It was winter in Sydney! We wound up going to the warmer Gold Coast, and we pitched a tent on the beach. Believe it or not, we lived in the tent for 10 years!

Our fortunes really turned around. I became the highest paid postcard model in Australia, and I earned a lot of money. Eventually I bought land in Byron Bay from doing a calendar. I still have it. I am lucky to have a lot of money now. I live in Hawaii, and still go to Australia, because two of my children are still there. One is in California. Every year I go around the world!

For a long time, it puzzled me why no one would pick us up on the highway through the Nullarbor. You would think that a woman with three small children, struggling along in the heat, would get immediate help.

I found out later from truck drivers that people passed us by because they thought I was the "Nullarbor Nymph"! This is a "woman" who looks human and walks across the Nullarbor. Truck drivers pick her up and take her thousands of miles. She helps them stay awake by talking to them, and when they get close to where they are going to drop her off, she suddenly disappears. She is blonde and wears red shoes. I was blonde and was wearing red high-heeled shoes. If she's a spirit or ghost, she must be a good one to keep truckers awake, but let's face it, most people are scared of ghosts. Aren't they?

Commentary
B.B. has plenty of company – throughout history, certain people have been shunned because others thought they were supernatural, and therefore dangerous. Usually anything that distinguishes an "outsider" makes a person a candidate. In earlier times, fair-haired people in a land of dark-haired people would be considered witches and dangerous. Likewise, red hair (an unusual trait in most places) is a marker. Dangerous spirits are often described as wearing red clothing, caps, and shoes.

In addition, widespread lore about dangerous female hitchhikers has existed for centuries. In Spanish lore, La Llorona brings death to some of those who give her a ride. Sometimes, she merely disappears along the route. In American ghost lore, "Resurrection Mary" is a young girl who died from being struck by a car while she walked along a road at night. Her ghost hitches rides to her family home or to the cemetery where she is buried (Resurrection Cemetery outside of Chicago), and disappears from the back seat when the destination is reached. Similar phantom hitchhiker motifs fall under the category of urban legend.

Even though some of these legendary phantom and supernatural hitchhikers are benign, individuals who know the stories could certainly be put off by someone who fits the description, even in modern times.

The Nullarbor Nymph has an interesting twist, however – the story began as a hoax. Reports of a half-naked, blonde white woman living among kangaroos in the Nullarbor Plain surfaced in the Australian media in 1971-72. The first reports were made by professional kangaroo shooters from Eucla (a town of population eight), who had a poor quality video showing a woman holding a kangaroo by the tail. The story quickly spread around Australia and the world.

One of the shooters confessed to the hoax in 1972, and said it had been created by a media publicist who passed through Eucla and stayed at the hotel there. The female in the film was a model, and another woman also was used for a photograph given to the media.

Despite the confession, the story had already become fixed in urban legend and popular folklore, and it took on a real life of its own. Its authenticity was further established by a 2012 low-budget Australian film, The Nullarbor Nymph, *which received a great deal of attention and positive reviews.*

The Nullarbor Nymph is not the first hoax to become real. In the late nineteenth to early twentieth centuries, hoax adventure stories were created by competing newspapers as a way of garnering readers. Many had supernatural content. The failing Middletown Valley Register *newspaper in Maryland started a Snallygaster hoax, involving a flying dragon-like creature that attacked people, especially children, and drank their blood. People believed it and continued to believe it after the hoax was exposed. Sightings of the monster were reported in several states – and continue to this day.*

In 2009, Slender Man was created as a creepypasta Internet meme. Tall, gaunt, pale, and dressed in black, Slender Man attacks and terrorizes children. Slender Man also took on a life of its own, and encounters with this entity are reported all over the globe. Never mind that it started as a fiction – it is all too real now.

B.B. Dupre learned this strange lesson of the supernatural landscape the hard way. Fortunately, her story had a happy ending.

THE ROADSIDE COWBOY
Joe Redmiles

An odd figure materializes on a suddenly deserted highway.

In October 2015, my wife (Rosemary Ellen Guiley) and I were driving through Arizona. We were returning to Phoenix from Sedona in the evening, after visiting friends. We had an early flight out of Phoenix the next day and planned to stay the night in a hotel near the airport. We had stayed for several days in Sedona, where we had discussed skinwalkers, UFOs, tricksters, and other paranormal weirdness with our friends.

My experience happened about 9:30 PM. We were southbound on I-17, the major freeway connecting points north and south. We had made this drive many times, but tonight things felt different. The air around us felt electrically charged and very active. Rosemary also noticed how weird the atmosphere felt and we talked about this a bit. I was driving about 10 miles per hour under the speed limit because

I felt a need to be extra cautious. I did not want to be stopped for speeding or any other reason.

We passed through a particularly dark and desolate stretch of highway. There were no other cars in sight, which was strange for a Sunday night – a lot of people travel between Phoenix and Sedona on the weekends.

Something on my right caught my eye. I looked closer and saw that there was a light about 75 yards off from the road. I noticed a dirt road leading back into the distance, which I assumed was someone's driveway. Standing at the head of this driveway was a man dressed in a cowboy shirt, jeans, and boots. He was tall and thin and looked about 70 years old. He had a thick, full, "Sam Elliot" type of mustache. He was very fit and stood straight and tall. There was an "old-fashioned" look to him.

This man was facing the freeway. His left arm was cocked, hand on his waist. His right arm was fully extended and in his right hand he held a light, which seemed to be a Coleman lantern. He was watching the freeway, stone-faced, and standing stock still. I knew that he was watching us – almost like he was expecting us.

I wondered, *What in the world is this old guy doing, standing out here on the freeway at this time of night, alone, just watching and waiting?* In a matter of a few seconds he was out of sight as we continued south. I told Rosemary what I saw, but by then we were long past the spot, She said she had not seen the figure, even though it was on the same side of the road as the passenger seat. I wondered how she could have missed him and his lantern light.

I should also mention that shortly before I saw this man, Rosemary noticed some dark, large shapes moving about in the highway median. Earlier, I'd also been aware of dark shadows flying across the road but thought them only tricks of the eye, until I had the "old man" encounter.

We both felt that the shadows might have been a kind of trans-dimensional encounter. But, who or what was the old man with the lantern? I felt that he was more than real, but was he a ghost, or another part of our trans-dimensional experience?

Commentary

Roadside mystery figures are a frequently reported phenomenon, especially when travelers are alone on the road at night. Are they ghosts – or something else? Sedona, and many parts of Arizona, host all kinds of mysterious things. Tricksters figure prominently in the Native American lore.

The cowboy figure seemed out of place, not only in location, but in time. Although the light was bright and the figure quite distinct, Joe was the only one who saw it. That, too is common: one person sees something strange while others do not.

It could be argued that a real person was standing by the freeway with a light, waiting for someone who was expected, and who might miss the turnoff. It's plausible, but not likely.

It is not likely, either, that the cowboy was a residual ghost, for Joe had the distinct impression that it looked right at him in an expectant way.

Perhaps it was an unknown or trickster figure, making an appearance for unfathomable reasons. The earlier conversations about such figures could have primed the pump for an experience to happen. It is interesting that the environment seemed charged and weird – and suddenly devoid of traffic. Dark shadows were about. Such phenomena are a prelude to an opening between worlds, when a highway stops being a highway and becomes a "road to strange."

THE INSTANT DOWNLOAD
Richard Dickison

An out-of-body experience and telepathic contact with a mysterious being lead to a life-long mystical quest.

I lived in Japan in the mid-1970s. I was sitting at home one day reading a book, when I had a spontaneous out-of-body experience. I was transported to somewhere – I have no idea where – and I was standing in front of an entity that had a humanoid outline but no details: I could see a head and shoulders but no arms or legs.

This entity was communicating with me in some sense, but I didn't understand. It didn't involve words. Rather, it involved more of an instantaneous transfer of information of which I can recollect nothing. I was overwhelmed and awed by the intensity of the experience. But, oddly, I had this feeling of love... although love is not adequate to describe the type of feeling, but it's the closest thing you can come to in English. If I could compare it to anything, the only way I could describe it – you've heard the term "drinking from a fire hose" – it was more like drinking from Niagara Falls!

I'm not a religious person at all. I wasn't taking any substances to create hallucinations, and this communication… one of the aspects that impressed me was that it was a *perfect* communication. That is, this entity was communicating with me better than I can communicate with myself! A lot of information was exchanged, like encyclopedias upon encyclopedias upon encyclopedias of information. I just stood there and went, *Wow!*

After this whole thing was over I sat there and cried for about half an hour at the intensity of it all. Even though more than 40 years have passed, if I sit there and think about it, it still brings tears to my eyes.

I have no idea why this experience happened, and I cannot remember even a bit of all that information that was exchanged. It was just a highly emotional, highly intense, awe-inspiring glimpse of something.

It did prompt me to do some exploring, and I'm still doing that. One of my interests now is the nature of consciousness, because I'm sure this had something to do with my consciousness going places where other consciousnesses seldom go. I was seeing things that others seldom see, and it has become a lifelong quest to figure out what the nature of that was. I'm doing all sorts of research, reading books on consciousness, and getting other people's perspectives of similar things, so that I can not only see my own perspective of it, but also see how others perceive their own similar experiences. I can get a broader picture of what's going on, and not just my own experience.

I want to understand what is the nature of reality. I don't yet, but it's a quest that one will never get bored of. A lot of people would say I already know on that deeper level. It's just that at this conscious level, I need better access to that level that knows.

Commentary
Richard's experience is being reported with increasing frequency in metaphysical, paranormal, and even UFO literature. The "download" consists of a short, intense reception of massive amounts of information in an energy that floods into the body and even feels capable of overwhelming the recipient. Sometimes there is a being who does the

downloading, and is described as an angel, extraterrestrial, "energy being," spirit guide, Ascended Master, light being, and so on, depending on the interpretation of the experiencer. Sometimes the download seems to come from a cosmic source, such as the Source of All Being. Feelings of love, awe, and wonder are common, and the recipient feels engaged in a transcendent experience.

Even though exact bits of information may not be recalled, the download usually activates something within the individual, such as a burst of creativity, inspiration, and ideas, or a search for deeper spiritual knowledge. Some people feel physically changed. These outcomes seem to be the real purposes of a download, and not the actual bits of information. Many recipients feel the information penetrates deeply into their consciousness and becomes available in pieces when the time is appropriate.

Downloads can be triggered by altered states of consciousness; intense spiritual study, meditation, and discipline; physical and emotional trauma; out-of-body experiences; and contact experiences such as with angels and aliens. They can take place in waking consciousness, altered states, and lucid dreams. Downloads are spontaneous, and may happen only once during a lifetime. Some people experience a "heavy" download, and then, over a period of years, smaller downloads that are more like flashes of inspiration and "knowing."

Experiences like Richard's open people to ponder cosmic connections, life purposes, and the Great Mystery.

AFTERWORD

We hope you enjoyed our collection of paranormal travel tales, which reveal the hidden dimensions of being on the road. Perhaps you are wondering how you can increase your chances of having a paranormal experience during your own travels.

There are no hard and fast rules, for paranormal experiences happen due to unique combinations of circumstances: place, time, emotions, subtle energy, and, most important of all, the consciousness of the individual. People who are born with an extra helping of innate intuitive and psychic ability – which everyone has to some degree – are likely to have more paranormal experiences. Likewise, individuals who pursue spiritual studies, paranormal research and activities, and meditation make themselves better candidates. However, as this book demonstrates, the paranormal can pop on anyone, even skeptics and disbelievers.

There are things you can do to become a "better traveler." You must change from being a "tourist" to a "traveler." The American historian Daniel Boorstin, describes the key difference in his book *The Image: A Guide to Pseudo Events in America* (1961):

> The traveler was active; he went strenuously in search of people, of adventure, of experience. The tourist is passive; he expects interesting things to happen to him. He goes "sight-seeing."

The more you travel, the more you stop being a tourist and become a seasoned traveler. This is a natural evolution as you gain more confidence about being self-sufficient in strange places and cultures. The more you engage in the cultures you visit – by learning history, customs, spirituality, folklore, arts, and even a bit of the language – the more immersed you become in the "vibe" of the locale.

Thus, you learn the deeper experience of "living" and "experiencing" a culture instead of just touring, surviving, and satisfying

237

only the most basic of your travel needs. Safety and physiological needs come first, but if one fulfills the higher order needs such as love, belonging, self-esteem, and self-actualization, the over-all human experience that results from travel is far more rewarding.

Open yourself up to new experiences, be more sociable, entertain and embrace diversity, and pay more attention to the stimuli around you. Take more "time to smell the roses," as the adage goes. As you do so, you allow more of the universe – the multi-verse – to become manifest to you. That is the stuff that travel is all about.

Send us your paranormal travel stories!

We're planning more volumes, and we'd like to hear from you. We're interested in travel experiences involving paranormal phenomena; ghosts and hauntings; visions; psychic experiences; time slips; past lives; déjà vu; synchronicity; mysterious creatures and beings; UFOs and aliens; crop circles; sacred sites, mystical experiences; and more.

Stories can be of any length. We reserve the right to edit them to fit the style and format of our books. Stories will be credited to the authors. As a thank you, we will send you an autographed copy of the book.

Please send your stories to either Michael Brein at michaelbrein@ gmail.com or Rosemary Ellen Guiley at reguiley@gmail.com.

Thank you and happy travels!

ABOUT THE AUTHORS

Michael Brein

Michael Brein is an author, lecturer, consultant, travel storyteller, adventurer, and publisher of travel books and guides. He earned his PhD in social psychology, with a specialty in psychology – all things travel – as well as an MBA at the University of Hawaii. He has had a career for more than 20 years as a college professor in psychology and business, teaching at a variety of universities in Hawaii, as well as an overseas two-year stint teaching for the University of Maryland in Europe.

Michael was the first to coin the term "travel psychology." Through his doctoral studies, work, life experiences, and world travels, he became the world's first and perhaps only travel psychologist. As "The Travel Psychologist," he appears in leading newspapers, magazines, blogs, and radio programs all over the world, commenting on the psychology of travel. Among his media credits are: *USA Today, Conde Nast Traveler, Inquisitr, The Thrillist, The Scientific American, The Huffington Post,* and many more.

Michael has been a member of a number of world travel clubs, among them the Travelers Century Club, whose requirement for membership is travel to a minimum of 100 countries, and the Circumnavigators Club, which requires going around the world in one complete trip.

He was the first to complete the United Airlines "50 State Marathon" contest in 1985, flying to all 50 U.S. states to win a first-class pass for a year on United's domestic U.S. flights, including Hawaii.

Michael's travel guide series, *Michael Brein's Travel Guides to Sightseeing by Public Transportation,* is a first of its kind, showing travelers how to sightsee the top 50 visitor attractions in the world's most popular cities easily and cheaply by public transportation.

Michael has traveled the world over for the past four decades interviewing nearly 1,800 world travelers and adventurers, collecting their fantastic travel stories for an e-book and audiobook series on the psychology of travel.

Finally, Michael has been the State Director for Hawaii and Ambassador-at-Large for MUFON (the Mutual UFO Network), the largest UFO research organization in the United States with a significant worldwide presence as well.

Michael resides on Bainbridge Island, Washington. His website is www.michaelbrein.com, and email is michaelbrein@gmail.com.

Rosemary Ellen Guiley

Rosemary Ellen Guiley is one of the leading figures in the paranormal and metaphysical field – author, researcher, investigator, radio show host, and publisher. She has written more than 60 nonfiction books on a wide range of topics, including a series of authoritative single-volume encyclopedias. She is often the "go-to" person for explanations of unusual phenomena and events.

Her work focuses on extraordinary experiences of all kinds: paranormal, spiritual and mystical, contact with the dead, contact with otherworldly beings, and psychic breakthroughs.

Rosemary runs an independent publishing house, Visionary Living, Inc., which publishes paranormal, metaphysical, and ufology titles. She hosts a popular weekly live radio show, *Strange Dimensions*, on the KGRA Digital Broadcasting Network, and publishes a monthly newsletter by the same title. She is Executive Editor of *FATE* magazine.

In addition, Rosemary is a Tarot reader and intuitive consultant, and a dreamwork facilitator, helping people understand the meaning of their dreams.

Rosemary is a board director and member of the research committee of the Edgar Mitchell Foundation for Research Into Extraterrestrial Encounters, and is a board director and book review editor of the Academy for Spiritual and Consciousness Studies. She is a founding member of the Afterlife Research and Education Institute, and a fellow of the International Institute for Integral Human Sciences in Montreal.

Rosemary makes numerous media appearances and lectures internationally. She is a frequent guest on *Coast to Coast AM* with George Noory. She lives in Connecticut.

Her website is www.visionaryliving.com, and her email is reguiley@gmail.com.